The Business Guide to Insurance

The Business Guide to Insurance

Norman Lawrence

Croner Publications Ltd
Croner House
London Road
Kingston upon Thames
Surrey KT2 6SR
Telephone: 01–547 3333

Published by
Croner Publications Ltd,
Croner House,
London Road,
Kingston upon Thames,
Surrey KT2 6SR
Telephone: 01–547 3333

While every care has been taken
in the writing and editing of this book,
readers should be aware that only Acts of Parliament
and Statutory Instruments have the force of law,
and that only the courts can authoritatively
interpret the law.

British Library Cataloguing in Publication Data
Lawrence, Norman
1.   Great Britain. Business firms. Insurance
I.   Title
368

ISBN 1–85452–034–2

Phototypeset by Input Typesetting Ltd, London
Printed in Great Britain by Ebenezer Baylis & Son Ltd,
The Trinity Press, Worcester, and London

To my wife, Marie

Contents

Preface

The business or professional person seeking information about insurance today relies on the knowledge and integrity of the many insurance advisers available. Some of these are employed by insurance companies, others are intermediaries willing and able to offer independent advice. However, the public must be forgiven if they feel that a sale may be more important to the insurance vendor than the information he or she can provide. In fact, today, few people are prepared to put their trust entirely in an adviser whose worth they have not experienced for themselves.

The alternative for those seeking knowledge of insurance is to buy one of the many textbooks available in the bookshops. However these are of a technical nature and, although it is not beyond the ability of most people to master them, it is time consuming.

This book has tried to be different. There are answers to technical questions presented in a very readable way. The book can be used as a work of reference in which the business can find satisfactory answers to the many problems of insurance troubling it. Security against intruders, malicious persons and against fire are also of interest to the business and these aspects too are dealt with in a practical way.

Life insurance and house purchase, as well as insurances on the home and its contents are dealt with.

During a long working life spent in insurance, the author has both practised and taught insurance. Many questions have been put to him and some of these, together with the answers, have been incorporated in the text.

The author wishes to acknowledge the information supplied by the Association of British Insurers and the Loss Prevention Council. He is also grateful for the opportunity of examining the prospectuses and specimen policies kindly supplied by many of the leading insurers in Great Britain, including the Guardian Royal Exchange Assurance, the Commercial Union Assurance, the Eagle Star Insurance Company, the Cornhill Insurance, the Prudential Assurance Company, the General Accident, Fire and Life Assurance Corporation, the Municipal Mutual Insurance Company and the Norwich Union Insurance Group.

N. Lawrence
April, 1989.

CHAPTER 1

Introduction

What is insurance?

It may seem strange that a book which sets out to demonstrate to business people the need for, and the availability of, insurance protection commences with a question. However, before launching into details of the insurance cover available, it is important that the reader is asked to pause and consider what insurance really is, what it provides and — more importantly — what it can do for the business.

Trade and business are entered into with a view to making a profit. There are many risks inherent in this seemingly simple task. The trader risks buying the wrong goods, paying the wrong price for them, offering them in the wrong markets and at the wrong price. Competition may be good or bad, dependent on circumstances. What is certain is that fire, theft, vandalism, illness or physical injury to ourselves and innocent people around us will result in anxiety, grief and financial hardship.

Every day the newspapers and television demonstrate all the hazards that can befall any one of us. We have become used to most of the day to day events that fill the press. Those of us who still believe that they only happen to others have been very lucky indeed. Anyone can be the victim. So certain is it that we are all vulnerable that the term "Act of God" has almost vanished from use in the world of insurance. Even the advent of typhoons that wash away ships and hurricanes that destroy cities must be anticipated by those whose business it is to offer insurance. These people will be referred to as "insurers" in the text.

The risks that we run in our day to day affairs can be separated into two not very distinct groups. Some of them are insurable, but there are some that are not. The division between them is never clear cut. Whilst there are many risks that would not be acceptable to insurers there are borderline areas. In addition a particular hazard may be uninsurable in one generation, insurable in the next and then become uninsurable in the one after that. Public opinion and its effect on Government action is very often the cause. An example of this is insurance against legal liability. It was once felt that it would be wrong to allow people to insure against their own negligence, particularly if they broke the law at the same time. Thus, if someone caused injury to an innocent party as a result of bad driving then he or she should be forced to suffer. Insurance should not be available to alleviate this. For many years now third party motor insurance has been available and is, in fact, a compulsory requirement for those using a vehicle on a road. Yet, just prior to the last war the term "delinquent drivers" was used in an official report.

More recently insurance became available to provide a chauffeur driven car or a chauffeur to those who were banned from driving by the courts following certain convictions under the Road Traffic Acts. A Government commissioned review early in 1988 recommended that such policies should be void. The reaction of the Association of British Insurers, of whom you will read more later on, is to suggest to those who offer such insurance that they should remove cover for drink driving offences or risk having it made illegal.

What insurance seeks to do is to offer compensation against a loss. To be eligible for insurance it must be possible to calculate the possible loss in financial terms. A ring that has been in the family for many years is not insurable if it is only of sentimental worth and has no market value. The market value is what it is worth to others who might have bought it had it been for sale. Thus one insures for the cost of repairing or replacing the lost or damaged goods. Additionally, those who suffer injury and satisfy the courts that the injury resulted from our negligence will be awarded damages against us. It is possible to insure against this eventuality.

If a situation can be affected almost entirely by the personal element it is unlikely to be insurable. This eliminates what are known as speculative risks: things like pricing a product or entering a new market. In these cases individual business acumen affects the outcome. In practical terms, unless similar impersonal risks exist in sufficient numbers, insurers are unlikely to offer cover. Occasionally an insurer may be prepared to quote terms to accept a risk that is highly individual. Certainly individual risks are offered to Lloyd's underwriters daily.

The purpose of insurance is to put an insured person back into the same position as he or she was in, prior to the loss. In many cases this can only be carried out in approximate terms. It would be against public policy if insured persons were able to make a profit out of a fire or a theft. If one is talking about the insurance of life or limb then there must be an agreement as to the value of the possible loss when insuring. Thus individuals insure their lives for previously agreed sums of money.

If an insured is to be put into the same, or near enough the same, position as he or she was in prior to a loss then that person must be either the owner of the property insured, or responsible for it in such a way as to have a financial interest in its safety. This could arise when goods have been borrowed, whether payment has been made or not, or left for repair or cleaning. Without this interest, any insurance effected would be void.

Terms used in insurance

All businesses, trades and professions have a language of their own. Try as they may, practitioners eventually have to use the technical terms known to them to actually pin-point what it is that they want to say. Insurance is no exception. Much work is being done at the present time to produce what are called "plain English" policies. Most insurers have moved in that direction. Some have completely rewritten their proposal forms, policies and other documents. Others have made some concessions to the insuring public. The terms in general use remain because they have been accepted for many years, even centuries in most cases, and, during that time, the courts have decided precisely what they mean.

The insurer

In using the term "insurer" it is intended to refer to anyone whose business it is to offer cover against the risks discussed earlier. It could be a company owned by shareholders who expect the business to be run at a profit. In the case of life insurance, shareholders offer to share the profits made with those policyholders who are willing to pay a small extra premium for that privilege.

There are in existence insurers who do not have shareholders and are owned by the policyholders themselves. These are the mutual companies. Any profits made by them belong to the policyholders. In some cases funds are set up in certain trades in order to pay for losses that cannot be easily insured. Certain risks run by ship owners fall into that category and are met by what are known as "Protection and Indemnity Associations".

Another type of insurer is the Lloyd's underwriter. Very many misconceptions exist about them. They are individuals who accept proportions of insurance risks offered to them. They receive a proportion of the premium paid and pay a similar proportion of the losses. Each underwriter is responsible for his or her proportion and that proportion alone. However, they are not protected by limited liability as many traders are and could suffer the loss of their capital and their homes if misfortune were to strike.

Most of those who are called Lloyd's underwriters do not have the technical ability to underwrite insurance themselves. They merely lend their names to the risks they accept in the hope of making a profit. They join other underwriters to form "syndicates" which are managed for them. The managers of the syndicates employ experienced underwriters who are available in the room at Lloyd's in London, where the business is actually transacted, to consider, and accept or reject insurances offered. Policies issued at Lloyd's show the percentages of the risk accepted by each syndicate.

Lloyd's is not an insurance company. It does not transact insurance. It is, in effect, a private club in which the agents of those who seek insurance can meet those who are prepared to offer insurance and discuss their business, prepare the policies and deal with the claims that arise. Although technically only liable for their own share of any loss, all underwriters subscribe to a fund set up by Lloyd's to protect policyholders.

The proposer

Those who wish to insure are referred to as proposers. A proposer usually completes a form, called a proposal form, which is designed by insurers to answer the questions that will enable them to consider the proposition offered. Some types of insurance require more information than others. Some insurers ask many more questions than others. In the case of very large industrial insurances a proposal form is inappropriate and other means have to be employed to obtain the details of risks offered. When an insurance is accepted by the insurer the proposer becomes the insured under the contract entered into between them.

The underwriter

The word "underwriter" has been used above in discussing the procedures at Lloyd's. An underwriter is someone whose job it is to examine the information available to him or her about the insurance offered and decide whether to accept or refuse it. If the underwriter decides to accept, he or she will then calculate the premiums to be charged and the terms to be offered. It has been seen how Lloyd's operates but the underwriters employed by a company or mutual insurer are risking their employers' capital and not their own. They head departments specialising in particular classes of insurance. Their titles are marine underwriter, accident insurance manager or motor insurance superintendent. Most of the risks offered to their departments will be considered by underwriting staff using formulae laid down by them. Only very large or particularly difficult risks will be referred to them for their personal attention.

Insurance and assurance

There is one question that members of the public always ask those of us in the insurance world. That question is "What is the difference between insurance and assurance?"

The short answer is that there is no difference! Early traders in insurance used the term "assurance", which is of Italian origin. During the nineteenth century this word was taken to relate to situations in which insurers were bound to make a payment eventually, as in life insurance. However, many life insurers use the term "insurance" and at Lloyd's the term assurance is used in marine insurance practice. The word insurance is of much more recent origin and was originally used to refer to situations in which a payment may or may not be made during the currency of an insurance policy, as in fire or motor insurance.

Statutes in this country use the words "insurance" and "assurance" quite indiscriminately so that it can be safely said that there is no distinction between them, in present day practice.

In this handbook the words "insurance", "insured" and "insurer" will be used exclusively.

Broker

Once or twice the word agent has been used. In English law anyone who acts on behalf of another is an agent. In insurance the term "broker" has been used to differentiate between those whose main or only occupation was the transaction of insurance on behalf of others and those who had another main occupation but also transacted insurance. Included in the latter category were accountants, surveyors, garage proprietors and bank managers. For over 100 years the Corporation of Insurance Brokers pressed for the title broker to be available only to those qualified to undertake the task of advising about and placing insurance risks — very much in the same way as many other holders of professional titles, such as doctors, dentists and pharmacists are protected by law. Finally, in 1976 four associations united in preparing proposals to the Government which resulted in the Insurance Brokers' Registration Act 1977.

Since 1.12.81 it has been illegal for anyone who is not registered under the Act to call himself or herself an insurance broker. For the public it means that individual brokers must be registered and, in the case of limited companies, at least half the directors must be registered. In order to register a certain standard of technical knowledge is required, professional experience is essential and the financial status of the firm must be monitored. In addition members must carry professional indemnity insurance, which means that if they are negligent in their advice or actions their clients are indemnified by insurance. Recent events in the world of finance have aroused considerable interest in this feature.

The statement above must not be taken to mean that only those registered as brokers are able correctly to carry out the job of advising about insurance. There are experienced individuals and firms using the titles of "consultants", "financial advisers" and other similar terms who still refer to themselves as insurance agents. There are life insurance companies who employ representatives to transact insurance directly with the public. In some cases these are also referred to as "agents", although they are not strictly so.

In this handbook the term "intermediary" is used to describe those who act on behalf of the proposer in placing insurance business.

The peculiarity of insurance intermediaries is that they receive their remuneration, not from those who instruct them (as in other commercial agencies), but from the insurers with whom they place the business. In fact at some points in a transaction the law will hold that they are agents for the insurers and not the proposer.

Is insurance essential?

It has previously been established that insurance is available against a variety of risks. Without insurance how could one cope with the possibility of financial loss resulting from those risks that are often outside the trader's control? One suggestion, presumably, is to set aside a sum of money each year out of profits. If the value of the stock is a quarter of a million pounds perhaps it may be decided to commence a reserve by setting aside £2500 a year. Suppose a fire of serious proportions occurs after ten years? The reserve will be £25,000, plus accrued interest. A number of small losses may have further depleted the fund. The result, in practice, is that those businesses that suffer fire loss and have no insurance, or are inadequately insured or have fire insurance but are not covered for loss of income, go out of business.

Large organisations with premises spread around the country are in a better position to set up their own reserves. After all, they will argue, insurers make a profit. We can avoid contributing to that by self-insurance. Given that they must spend money on risk management experts, who analyse and assess potential business hazards, they may save money. Insurers, however, spread their risks over a cross section of business and trades. Insurance companies trade with each other and also seek insurance for their larger risks from specialists called reinsurers. In this way the risks are spread thinner and thinner over the entire country — and also abroad. Losses which could cripple even a substantial business have little effect on established insurers.

The sort of figure mentioned in the example above — £2500 — could well be the annual premium asked by insurers for the risk mentioned. For that sum a trader buys peace of mind, has no capital tied up against possible losses and knows all available funds can be used freely in the business. By carefully selecting the insurance needed the unforeseen and unexpected, if it occurs, will not reduce the trader to bankruptcy.

Insurers also employ surveyors specially trained in fire precautions.

In some cases they may have specialists available in particular industrial processes. Specialists in intruder protection will also be employed
and expert advisers on liability will be available. Their advice assists
the underwriter in deciding on acceptances and in seeking improved
protections. This is of great value to proposers and insureds. An
insurance surveyor called in early enough in the planning stages can
save a lot of expense for a trader. No charge is made for his or her
services.

The cost of insurance is one of the expenses of a business. In return
for this sum, called the premium, insurers promise to pay those losses
detailed in the policy of insurance. This is the document issued by
insurers to confirm the cover granted. Unfortunately few people read
their policies even if they are written in what is called plain English.
It is important for the trader to know what cover is essential, whether
all of it has been agreed by insurers (sometimes the insured is asked
to bear the first part of a loss — called an "excess") and if the policy
document accurately reflects that agreement. On so many occasions
insured's have assumed that this or that is covered only to be disap-
pointed and suffer financially when a loss takes place. The time to be
sure is when effecting the insurance and again when it is renewed. If
any changes are made during the currency of the policy, insurance
should be one of the first matters to be considered. Any changes likely
to affect the insurance should be notified immediately to insurers and
not delayed until renewal date.

To reduce the documentation involved in issuing a number of small
insurance policies, insurers provide packages. The advantages to the
insured are that all the documents of insurance are in one folder
making everything easier to find, one premium only is paid and the
insurances all renew on one date. Quite often all the separate types
of insurance may be covered by just one policy, thus reducing the risk
of gaps in cover.

Answering questions

Q My insurance is described as comprehensive. Does that mean that
all the risks I face in my shop are covered by the policy?

A No. The term comprehensive is an unfortunate one that has been
in use for many years. All it actually means is that the insurances
effected cover a number of different risks, eg fire, theft, legal liab-

ility. It is more convenient than having many separate policies but you are in the same position as with any other policy of insurance — you need to know exactly what it covers.

Q Do all insurers give the same cover? What I mean is that if I have a theft insurance with one company and I am offered one by another company will they be identical?

A The answer to that question is no. Insurers are in business and, just like others in business, they compete with each other. Some insurers issue policies that grant more cover than others. Some have exclusions that others do not. It is only by knowing what you want that you can find out if you are getting it. In general, as with the purchase of any other product or service, you only get what you pay for. If you want the best you must pay for it. If you are prepared to accept reductions in cover you can effect savings.

CHAPTER 2

Types of Insurance

Here you will find the various classes of insurance listed under the headings generally used by members of the public and insurance intermediaries. These are not necessarily the divisions used by insurers at the present time. For example, many insurers differentiate between commercial and personal business. This means that one department, the commercial department, underwrites an entire insurance for a trader. Previously, business insurances would be dissected and each type of cover underwritten separately in the different departments. Thus, the fire insurance would have been dealt with by the fire underwriters, the theft insurance by the theft underwriters and so on. Private house insurance will be dealt with in a department usually called the "personal lines department".

Fire insurance

The basic policy offered to commercial and industrial organisations is called the "Standard Fire Policy". The Lloyd's Fire Policy is very similar but has some slight differences in wording. Although described as fire insurance policies both include, in the standard form, cover that is not within the definition of fire. Fire involves actual ignition. In other words the object that is damaged or destroyed must have actually ignited. This would exclude scorching of materials placed too near heat.

During the nineteenth century fire insurance became more complex as newer and newer processes developed in the industrial world. Furthermore, insurance depends on accurate statistical information and fire insurers found the need to share their statistics on a reciprocal basis with their competitors. Co-operation eventually led to the foundation of the Fire Offices' Committee in 1868. This is now part of the

Association of British Insurers. The Fire Offices' Committee, among other things, standardised the cover granted by the fire policy which was available from its members, agreed the wordings of endorsements and had an agreement on premiums. All the leading insurers of the time joined the Committee and later new entrants to the fire insurance business either joined or endeavoured to compete in terms, conditions and premiums.

The Standard Fire Policy covers

1. *Fire*, excluding its own spontaneous fermentation or heating or its undergoing any process involving the application of heat.

   The wording used, in excluding spontaneous heating, only excludes the item that spontaneously ignites but not the subsequent spread of fire.

Example

A haystack suddenly burst into flames and before the fire could be extinguished it had destroyed a nearby farm building.

The fire was clearly the result of spontaneous combustion but the use of the term "its" restricted the exclusion to the haystack so that cover for the building was not affected and the farmer was able to claim for the cost of rebuilding it.

A fire may result from an explosion, but an explosion caused by fire is inadmissible under the Standard Fire Policy although it is covered by the Lloyd's Fire Policy.

The policy also excludes fires caused by earthquake, subterranean fire, riot, civil commotion, war, invasion, act of foreign enemy, hostilities, civil war, rebellion, revolution, insurrection or military or usurped power.

Example

Following an earthquake, a fire started in a building and the wind spread it to nearby buildings. Insurers did not pay the claim. The fire damage was not covered as it resulted from earthquake which is excluded.

Some of these exclusions can be accurately defined whilst others are not as clear as they might be. For example, the definition of riot has recently been amended by the Public Order Act 1986 to mean an incident involving at least twelve people intending to and actually initiating an act using force of a degree as to alarm someone of reasonable courage. Civil commotion is somewhere between a riot and a civil war and is an insurrection of the people not amounting to a rebellion. There must be tumult present.

If the fire results from heating processes — as, for example, in cooking or baking — the materials being heated would be excluded if they caught fire, but once again the use of the word "its" would enable a claim to be made for any spread of fire.

2. *Lightning*, whether fire results or not.
3. *There is a specific exclusion in the standard fire policy of explosion.* Destruction or damage by explosion is excluded whether the explosion is caused by fire or otherwise.

Subterranean fire could be volcanic in origin but could include a fire in a coal mine or oil well.

Example

Following a fire at the premises, an explosion blew out the windows. The claim for the replacement of the windows was excluded, being concussion and not fire damage.

More complex is the situation following a fire caused by an explosion. The fire damage is included but not the explosion damage. Similarly, if a fire causes an explosion, only fire damage is covered. The impossibility, in each of these two cases, of separating accurately the fire damage from the explosion damage results in some bargaining between the insured and the insurer at the time of a settlement.

The policy allows limited explosion cover in respect of what are described as "domestic boilers". These are boilers not used in trade processes (they could be used exclusively for central heating, supplying hot water for handwashing or in the canteen of a factory). The policy also allows cover for explosion of gas used for lighting or heating the building.

Insurers are willing to provide cover in respect of most of the hazards excluded from the standard fire policy or the Lloyd's fire policy. Cover is also available in respect of other hazards.

Those items of cover excluded from the fire policies mentioned above may be added for a small extra premium. They include:

(a) *Explosion*

Explosions occur in boilers but can also be caused by dust (as in corn mills) or flammable liquids (oil, spirits, paint) or in chemical factories, caused by the inter-action of different chemicals. Explosion of boilers is more properly covered by an engineering insurance as this also includes the essential inspections. However, the damage caused by the explosion to other parts of the factory may be covered. The wording of the policy is such that other equipment which should be insured under an engineering insurance is also excluded, unless insurers are informed that it is not otherwise insured.

(b) *Spontaneous combustion*

Insurers are not happy to provide this cover and so it is only available in a very few cases. Inherent vice in many products and poor stacking makes this quite a difficult proposition for insurance.

(c) *Riot and civil commotion*

Some areas and certain risks are not covered. A riot has a legal definition but many of the other perils included in the full wording are not accurately defined. This extension includes both fire damage and any other damage, such as explosion or wrecking and looting, caused by rioters.

As an extension of this cover it is possible to include criminal damage. This would include malicious damage of any sort (not only fire). The insured is normally required to accept responsibility for part of the loss and to the exclusion of theft cover.

Example

A foreign football team visited the town to play the local team. All the tickets had been sold well before the great day arrived. A group of late arrivals circled the area and realised that a block of houses backed on to the ground. They broke into one of the houses, crossed the garden and attempted to climb the wall at the rear.

In a court action it was subsequently held that this was a riot.

(d) *Earthquake and subterranean fire*

Earthquake tremors are felt in this country but any damage caused has been insignificant. Similarly with subterranean fires, although fires have taken place in coal mines or oil wells.

The following perils may also be the subject of additional perils cover:

(e) *Storm, tempest and flood*

The words "storm" and "tempest" are not accurately defined but are thought to be interchangeable in most circumstances and are, therefore, used together in insurance policies and endorsements. Flood is usually defined as water which has escaped from natural or artificial lakes, reservoirs, canals, dams or entering from the sea. In many cases it can result from storm or tempest so that the all embracing title of the endorsement is valuable. It is usual to require the insured to pay the first £15 (or even more) of the cost of repairs in respect of damage to buildings.

The usual exclusions are of goods in the open, fences and gates. Any damage resulting from frost, subsidence or landslip will be excluded.

(f) *Subsidence and landslip*

Included in the term "landslip" is damage resulting from heave. Damage caused by the bedding down of new structures, settlement of newly made ground and coastal erosion are excluded. In a claim for damage to swimming pools, patios, terraces, footpaths, drives, fences, hedges, boundary or garden walls these will only be accepted if damage has also taken place to the building, its outbuildings or garages.

It is usual to require the insured to make a substantial contribution towards the building claim. This could be £500 or £1000, or a percentage of the costs of the rebuilding involved.

(g) *Bursting or overflowing of water tanks, apparatus or pipes*

The cover is in respect of damage to the tanks, pipes or apparatus and the buildings following upon the bursting or overflowing and subsequent water damage. The condition of the pipes affects the way in which the claim is settled as does the general maintenance of the property. If the damage results from accidental leakage of the sprinklers that would be excluded from the endorsement. Here again, an excess of £15 or more is usually imposed to avoid having to deal with small claims.

(h) *Sprinkler leakage*
This is designed to cover the insured in respect of any damage which may result from the sprinklers leaking or operating due to a heat source that is not "fire" as understood by the wording of the fire insurance. Claims arise following a drop in temperature which freezes the water which later thaws and bursts a pipe. As premises may be closed over weekends or for Bank Holidays this form of cover is essential.

(i) *Impact damage*
Over the years a number of separate endorsements have been incorporated into this one endorsement. It is intended to deal with damage that may be caused to a building by aircraft or any aerial device (for want of a better term), horses or any other animal, motor vehicles or railway trains. The risk of damage from the air exists for all of us, that of motor vehicles depends on the proximity of the building to a road, how busy the road is and if the property is near a bend in the road.

Some endorsements include damage caused by falling trees or parts of trees, but in some cases that risk could form a separate endorsement.

Business interruption insurance

This type of insurance is also known as "loss of profits" or "consequential loss" insurance. The alternative terms describe what is intended to be covered by this insurance — namely, the loss of profit. This loss must result from an insured loss. If, for example, the loss results from a fire the fire insurance would reimburse the insured in respect of the damage it had caused to his or her premises, stock and any other insured items such as equipment, fixtures and fittings. Subject to having sufficient insurance all of these things can be replaced and the business continue as before. However, there has been another loss which has not been met and, indeed, is excluded from the fire insurance. That is loss as a consequence of the fire.

Immediately the fire has taken place the business has either ceased to trade or continues in a limited way. Certain costs must still be met such as mortgage interest, rates, the pay of salaried staff. In addition, and in an effort to reduce the loss, the insured may hire machinery or rent temporary premises. All of this will have an effect on the trading results for a limited period and will reduce the net profit of the business. Many years ago it was thought that the future profitability of a business was too nebulous as a subject of insurance. The situation and prospects of a business can be assessed from its trading accounts and this is used to produce, with reasonable accuracy, an estimate of the loss of revenue sustained by the business.

A proposer is usually asked to state the period of indemnity required. In many cases a period of indemnity of 12 months may be fixed by the policy. Few insurers are willing to accept insurance for a shorter period. If there is a fixed indemnity period it can usually be extended, if required, by payment of an additional premium. The period of indemnity is the period from the occurrence of the incident until the insured business is back to its pre-incident situation. The proposer's decision should be based on the nature of his or her business, the possibility of obtaining temporary machines or premises and how long it would take before his or her trade would return to the pre-incident level.

The causes of the loss of turnover need not only be a fire at the insured premises but also any of the hazards listed in the endorsements mentioned above, or following a break-in. There are situations in which fire or other insurable hazard elsewhere could bring the business to a halt and these too may be insurable.

Calculation of the loss under a business interruption insurance is among the more difficult claims to settle. Quite often accountants, rather than claims adjusters, are necessary. This is discussed in more detail in the section dealing with claims.

Example

In the early hours of Monday morning Charles was called to

his shop in the High Road. A fire had completely gutted the premises. His immediate need was to find temporary premises nearby so as to retain his customers. The loss of stock and the cost of repairs, he knew, were covered by his fire policy. His worry was about being able to pay his outgoings.

The loss adjuster instructed by the insurers told him that the claim under his business interruption insurance covered the wages of his two staff, the interest on the overdraft and his rent — if he is still liable to pay it. Without business interruption insurance he would have been out of business in spite of having fire insurance.

Theft insurance

Theft insurances in the past were dealt with in the burglary department. From 1916 the legal definitions were of burglary and house-breaking. The Theft Act 1968 changed the terms in use and produced a legally defined term "theft".

The first section of the Act defines theft as "dishonestly appropriating property belonging to another with the intention of permanently depriving the other of it". "Permanently depriving" is a very important term to note in this context. Certainly if the "thief" parts with the property after "stealing" it or sells or tries to sell it, then it should be possible to prove theft.

Burglary involves entry to a building as a trespasser with the intent to commit certain offences. Among the offences is that of stealing or attempting to steal. It also includes stealing after entry as a trespasser. If a weapon or explosives are carried then the activity becomes "aggravated burglary". There is also a definition of robbery which involves the use of force or the threat of actual violence before or at the time of stealing.

The term "theft" is too wide for insurance purposes as it would include pilferage or shoplifting. The definition of a trespasser could include someone who enters a prohibited part of the premises (eg a stock room). Insurance policies, therefore, define the cover offered. As an example the wording may be:

> "theft involving entry to or exit from the premises by force" or "theft following forcible and violent entry".

The terms "forcible" and "violent" are used in most cases to clarify the situation. Earlier wordings (prior to the 1968 Act) used the words "breaking and entering". Even turning a door handle was construed as "breaking and entering". The wordings in use today do not include the use of a key (either a copy or a skeleton), entry by a trick or hiding on the premises and leaving without using force (eg awaiting re-opening).

The policy may include hold-up or the extra cover is available upon payment of an additional premium. Damage to the building caused by forcible entry or exit or attempted entry will be covered if the property is not owned by the insured. If the building is the property of the insured, damage caused by thieves would be given under the buildings insurance.

There is an exclusion of theft or collusion by staff or one of the insured's family.

In cases in which all the stock, or even a major part of it, is unlikely to be stolen by thieves (perhaps due to the weight of each item) insurers may agree to insure for partial value only. This is known as "first loss" insurance. The insured is still required to declare the total sum insured and up-date it as necessary. The cost of insurance will only be cheaper if the sum covered is to be for a lot less than the total stock.

Some trades are regarded as hazardous because of the value of the items involved in proportion to their size (eg jewellery), because of the ease of disposal (eg cigarettes and tobacco and clothing), or because of the special attraction of the goods (eg videos, cassette recorders).

In some cases insurers may insist on special protections, such as intruder alarms, before acceptance of the risk.

Many insurers require the insured to be responsible for the first £50 of any loss. This is referred to as "£50 excess". Excesses are used by insurers to avoid having to deal with small claims because the cost of handling the claim could be far greater than the amount claimed.

All risks

The difference between "comprehensive" and "all risks" may need clarification at this point. The term comprehensive is merely used to show that the cover granted by the policy relates to more than one class of insurance (eg a motor insurance covering third party and accidental damage; a household insurance covering fire and theft). An all risks insurance covers almost all the risks that can befall the items insured. The practice is to list those hazards that are excluded which, apart from those usually applied to insurance, are the obvious ones, such as wear and tear, gradual deterioration or damage caused by vermin or moth. In addition, electrical and mechanical breakdown are excluded.

Cover may be restricted to a specified address or may be anywhere in the United Kingdom or Europe. Most traders' insurances provide protection against fire and theft but it is possible today to obtain accidental damage cover. This would extend the benefits of "all risks" cover to fixtures and fittings owned by the tenant (owners of buildings could extend their existing buildings insurance) and include items like neon and electric signs.

If the contents insurance does not include accidental damage cover for business equipment, business all-risks insurance may be obtained. This could cover, for example, such items as cash registers, scales or microcomputers against accidental damage (eg equipment dropped) or theft from the premises at any time. It will be noted that pilfering and shoplifting are not covered by a theft insurance.

Example

After a particularly busy day in the shop the staff began the job of clearing up. Someone noticed that the 14 inch colour monitor was missing from the personal computer being used to display decor. A search took place but it was realised that sometime during the late afternoon the monitor had vanished. Later that evening the manager checked the policy cover to find that a theft claim required proof of "visible and forcible entry". His worries ceased when he found that there was also cover for specified business equipment in respect of loss or damage. The endorsement on the policy confirmed cover, subject to a £50 excess.

Miscellaneous theft insurances

There are many situations in which either the standard theft policy is not available or it is inappropriate. Examples are:

(a) *Club-houses and pavilions*
These are generally isolated and of non-standard construction and not looked upon favourably by insurers. Members' private effects may be covered, subject to quite low limits. Cups and trophies must be kept in a securely locked place. Stocks of spirits, wine, beer and tobacco must be kept low.

(b) *Churches*
Communion and church plate must be kept in a locked safe in the vestry with cover extended to use in the vicarage, church-warden's house or other private dwelling. The plate may be insured on an all risks basis or in respect of forcible entry only. Damage to premises may or may not be given but damage to stained glass windows is usually excluded.

(c) *Exhibitions*
The cover would be on a short-period basis. Insurers would specify a maximum value for any single item, as well as the maximum sum insured. The type of exhibition, the premises and whether they are occupied will affect acceptance and premium.

All these risks will be enhanced, from the insurer's point of view, if adequate arrangements are made for security. This could range from security on the premises to regular calls by a security firm.

Money insurance

This is an "all risks" cover in respect of money which is defined so as to include cheques, postage and trading stamps, credit card vouchers, VAT vouchers and luncheon vouchers.

A number of separate risks are covered. They are in respect of money:

(a) on the premises during business hours or carried by the insured

or his or her employees or sent by post (subject to a limit which
may be £3000);

(b) in the bank's night safe (limit as above);

(c) on the premises:

   (i) in a locked safe (on the premises or at the home of employer
       or employees) out of business hours (usually about £1000);

   (ii) from the home of employer or employees (maximum when
        occupied — £500, when unoccupied — £300).

Cover in respect of crossed cheques and similar items may be as high
as £250,000. There may or may not be an excess.

Losses resulting from the dishonesty of employees is covered by a
fidelity guarantee insurance. However, it is usual to include cover in
respect of theft by employees but specifying that the theft must be
discovered within two or three days of it taking place.

The other main exceptions are:

(a) shortages due to error and omission;

(b) loss as a result of a key or combination codes to a safe being left
    on the premises;

(c) confiscation, nationalisation or other act of Government.

Assault cover is often given, or available, to provide benefit if an
employer or employee sustains bodily injury as a result of theft or
attempted theft. Although insurers specify these benefits, most are
willing to quote an additional premium in order to increase them.

The benefits stated in the policy are usually:

(a) death or loss of a limb or an eye or permanent total disable-
    ment — £5000;

(b) temporary total disablement, limited to two years' benefit — £50
    per week.

In addition there will be a benefit in respect of damage to clothing or
personal effects of £250.

The premium charged for money insurance is based on the amount
of money in transit annually. This is called "annual carryings". An
estimate is made at the beginning of each insurance period and
adjusted when actual figures are available.

If large sums of money are to be moved regularly (eg to pay wages
on a site or to bank) insurers will want to know the route taken, the
number of cars used and how many staff are involved. They will insist
that the time and the route vary from week to week.

Goods in transit insurance

The risk of pilferage has increased enormously over the years making it important that cover is obtained in respect of all goods being sent from one place to another. Cover is required for those who carry goods — their own or those of others — and those who send goods by road, rail, sea or air. In the case of air or sea transport, insurances may be obtained from the marine insurance department of an insurance company.

If the insured uses his or her own vehicle or is in the haulage business the sum insured would be based on the maximum load with a possible single item limit. Special policies are available for furniture removers and for those whose furniture is to be removed.

Cover is practically all risks and is for loss or damage to goods by fire, theft, accident or pilferage whilst being loaded on, carried by or unloaded from the insured vehicle. Included is cover whilst the vehicle is temporarily garaged during transit. The standard policy is usually restricted to Great Britain.

Apart from the usual exclusions relating to radioactive contamination, the standard exclusions are:

(a) war, riot, civil commotion, earthquake or subterranean fire;
(b) moth, vermin, insects, damp, dew, mildew or rust;
(c) delay, loss of market, consequential loss, deterioration and changes by natural cause;
(d) theft or pilferage assisted, brought about or connived at by the insured's employees.

The consequential loss exclusion would protect insurers against claims for losses not relating to the goods themselves but due to the effect of the loss of the goods, eg loss of the expected profit, loss of a contract resulting from the incident, or effect of the loss on future trading or contracts.

Certain types of goods are excluded from standard policies, either because they are inherently dangerous or have a value that is high in relation to their bulk. Obtaining cover for some of them could be difficult. They include:

explosives, acids, bullion, cash, currency, deeds, bonds, securities, jewellery, precious stones, clocks, watches, curios, antiques, patterns, designs and livestock.

There may be an excess applied to the policy, except for fire claims.

The premium is affected by the nature of the goods normally carried (susceptibility to damage or theft is important), security devices fitted to the vehicle (insurers usually impose requirements in this respect) and limit per load. Due to the special difficulties encountered in this field, insurers are very keen to have details of previous claims.

Where goods are being sent by road, rail or post, the influencing factors are the nature of the goods, their susceptibility to damage or theft, the limit per consignment and the method of transit used. Premiums may be based on annual transit or, where occasional transit is involved, on a single item basis. There are a number of schemes available for goods sent by post, most of which are cheaper to use than registered post for items of value.

Contractors' all risks insurance

A great deal of money is invested in new buildings or in the building of new roads, motorways and bridges. There are many varied risks involved. A major risk is that of damage to the work before it is finally accepted by the principal. Additional risks involve damage during the maintenance period, following completion of the work, which may be 12 months. Any of this may necessitate additional construction or reconstruction work, with consequential delays in completion of the project. The insurance reimburses the contractor in respect of loss following most of the perils discussed earlier in this chapter.

The insurance also provides cover in respect of materials, plant and other property brought to the site by the contractor. Such property is quite often subject to theft and malicious damage. Substantial excesses are usually negotiated except in respect of loss by fire and extra perils.

The contractor's liability is specified in special contract wording used by the Institute of Civil Engineering and the Royal Institute of British Architects.

Plate glass insurance

Accidental breakage or malicious breakage of exterior and interior glass in a building can be covered by insurance. This includes glass shelves and mirrors. Special premiums are charged for glass that is bent, painted, stained, tinted, embossed or lettered as well as for glass incorporated in multiple glazing units or which is frameless on any side.

It is usual to include cover in respect of frames and for displays damaged by the breakage. Most insurers have arrangements with specialist glaziers who will measure and board up where necessary and replace the glass rapidly. The glaziers will replace the broken glass with glass of a similar type, the salvage becoming the insurer's property. The alternative is for the insurers to pay the insured the current value of the glass less the value of the salvage.

It is the replacement service offered in glass insurance that makes it such a valuable one for the business person.

Liability insurance

This class of insurance is concerned with indemnifying an insured in respect of any payments he or she may have to make to a third party. That third party could be an employee or ex-employee who alleges that injury or disease was caused by his or her employer's negligence. The press has highlighted cases in which employers have become liable for substantial damages following death allegedly caused by industrial disease. A claim could arise from a member of the public who alleges injury resulting from the negligence of the occupier of a property. It could arise from a defect in premises or in goods sold or work undertaken.

Not all claims succeed but defending them can also be costly and there may not be any recompense in respect of the expenses involved. Insurers not only deal with the claim made but also pay the costs of defending any action against an insured. A high percentage of claims made are dealt with by negotiation and never reach the courts. However, even that aspect can be time consuming and costly.

Liability insurance may be sub-divided into:

(a) Liability to employees. This type of insurance is compulsory (except for some limited exemptions) under the Employers' Liability (Compulsory Insurance) Act 1969.

(b) Liability to members of the public who suffer injury as a result of the negligence of the insured or his or her employees. This could take place on or off the insured premises or on the premises of customers during deliveries or whilst work is in progress.

There are both common law and statutory liabilities (under the Occupiers' Liability Acts 1957/84). This class of insurance is referred to as public liability insurance.

(c) Liability for injury, illness, loss or damage resulting from the supply of goods. This is known as product liability insurance. The Consumer Protection Act 1987 specifies the liability of importers and manufacturers.

(d) Liability of professional people in respect of claims which could be made against them for negligence causing injury or loss to third parties. This class of insurance is usually called professional indemnity insurance (although the term professional liability insurance may be found in practice).

In addition many insurances include some form of third party liability in their cover. The liability aspects of these insurances will be dealt with when explaining the cover available. Examples are Motor Insurance, Household Insurance and Travel Insurance.

Each of the sub-divisions above will be examined separately below.

Employers' liability

An employers' liability insurance provides an indemnity to an insured in respect of damages, costs and expenses incurred in settling a claim in or out of court from an employee alleging bodily injury or disease caused by the employer's negligence. Misconceptions exist about liability insurance. The existence of a legal liability applies to all of us. Insurance is to provide for the payment of damages and the legal costs incurred. Legal costs may arise even where liability is later not proved against the insured or is non-existent. It cannot always be recovered from the third party.

Some parts of an employee's claim may not be insured, such as damage to clothing, but the employer is, of course, still liable. In practice insurance for this aspect is possible under the public liability insurance. Legislation enabling an injured employee, or his or her dependants in the event of his or her death, to claim against a negligent employer has existed since early in the nineteenth century. Until the introduction of the Employers' Liability (Compulsory Insurance) Act 1969 no attempt was made to deal with the fact that all employers could not afford to pay the damages awarded against them.

The Act makes it compulsory for an employer to insure in respect of the legal liability for bodily injury or disease to an employee. The amount of the cover must be at least £2 million. Most policies issued are unlimited in amount. In addition, the Act requires an employer to exhibit at each of his or her places of business a certificate issued by the insurer as proof of the existence of insurance.

Employees are all those who have a contract of service (whether in writing, oral or implied) with an employer and include apprentices. An employer does not have to insure in respect of domestic servants, most relatives or overseas residents employed for less than 14 days in Great Britain.

Example

John had been using the machine for almost six months. Much of the time he had been under the eagle eye of Mr Brown. Today Mr Brown was occupied with a new trainee and at last John was working on his own. Only the day before, the type of timber in use had been changed and appeared to be more resistant to the blade. However, John found that a little extra push here and there helped it through the blade. As he speeded up his work his hand was getting nearer and nearer the blade. Mr Brown called across "Are you OK, John?". To which John replied in the affirmative. Just three more pieces to insert and it would be time for a break . . .

What exactly happened, nobody — not even John — knew. The surgeon could not save two of John's fingers.

The claim in respect of the loss of two fingers did not go to court. The insurers and the trade union's solicitors reached an agreement.

An employer has a duty to provide competent fellow workers with safe and adequate equipment, a safe system of work, a safe place of work and access to it. In the example above the claim against the employer could have been based on a defect in the machine, poor "housekeeping" (perhaps oil on the floor causing it to become slippery), incorrect use of the machine (for example, removal of a guard, even if forbidden), insufficient training or insufficient supervision (especially of a trainee).

The Employers' Liability (Defective Equipment) Act 1969 makes an employer liable for injuries caused by defective equipment. He or she cannot deflect the claim to the manufacturer of the machinery or equipment. This does not prevent the employer taking action, in turn, against the manufacturer. This is not always possible if a manufacturer is no longer in business or difficult to sue in a foreign court.

There are other problems faced in settling employees' claims. Employers are not keen on adverse publicity. The media tends to select parts of a court action to report. The selected part may not show the employer in a good light. Examples are a heading in inverted commas to show it is a quote from a statement. The subtlety of the inverted commas may be missed by the average reader who just notices "poor conditions at local factory". He or she does not continue to the words "alleges solicitor". This means in practice that many claims are settled on "nuisance" value.

The premium is calculated on the annual wage and the type of work performed by the employee. Where there are many employees, the division may simply be between clerical and factory staff. The premium for clerical workers is low and the premium (calculated as a rate per cent of wages) is high for builders. In the case of building and demolition the maximum height worked is relevant. Some workers, in the building trade, are simply plasterers working in buildings in safer circumstances than, say, a tiler out on the roof.

Premiums are usually based on estimates and adjusted at the end of each period of insurance when actual wages paid are declared.

Public liability

The insurance is to reimburse the insured in respect of compensation he or she may pay to a member of the public as a result of personal injury or damage to property caused by his negligence or the negligence of his employees. As in employers' liability it is usual for the insurer to take over and deal with the claim from the third party on the insured's behalf.

There are many ways in which liability can arise. It can be caused by defects on the premises such as slippery floors, damaged floor coverings, defects on stairways and escalators, faulty passenger lifts, display units, goods falling from displays or shelves, hanging signs, trap-doors and many other situations. It is usual to insure lifts, hoists and escalators under engineering policies which provide maintenance and inspection, as well as insurance for legal liability.

In addition to those hazards listed above, there are the problems of pollution, certain external risks where extractors are in use, work carried out off the premises and deliveries.

Example

Martin and his brother Paul trading as "M & P Panel Beaters" worked from a small building on the far side of the corporation car park. The paint shop in the building had an extractor fan so that fumes could be removed from it. Due to an unexplained defect, a number of persons parking near M & P's building complained of paint spots on their cars. On investigation it was found that almost twenty cars in the car park had suffered in this way.

Insurers dealt with claims from the individuals concerned in respect of repainting and temporary hire of alternative transport. In some cases claimants employed solicitors and the claim included their costs too. The sum insured under M & P's public liability policy was sufficient to pay all the claims that had arisen.

Most public liability policies are issued for sums of £500,000 to £1M although it is possible to obtain higher sums. Claims made against those in the chemical industry show the need for much higher sums insured. Insurers and intermediaries will offer advice based on the size of claims being experienced in a particular trade. This is one area where insufficient insurance can be expensive.

Example

A large warehouse became vacant and Smith decided to rent it and convert it into a market. On the opening day a large crowd arrived and all seemed well. Screams from the direction of the ladies' room brought the security officer running and he was surprised to see three indignant and annoyed, but uninjured, ladies peering from a hole in the floor. Later inspection revealed that the bolts on a trapdoor concealed by the floor covering had broken allowing the ladies, who were standing in front of a mirror, to fall three feet through the opening.

Fortunately there were no injuries involved and insurers were able to settle by payments for damaged shoes, tights and one torn coat.

If an insured accepts additional liabilities in a contract to those he or she may have in common law, insurers would wish to be informed and may require an extra premium.

Insurers do not pay claims for defective workmanship. This means that if work is carried out badly and damage results, insurers will not be responsible for the cost of rectifying the damaged work. Any claim by third parties arising out of the incident would be covered.

It is not always possible to provide a clear demarcation between defective workmanship and legal liability. One example is that if a glazier is replacing a window and breaks the glass in the process insurers will not pay for replacement glass but they will pay for any other damage. If, however, in the process of repairing one window the glazier breaks another, that other would be a public liability claim. It can be seen that there are other possibilities involved that would need to be settled by negotiation.

Example

The furniture stores sent its driver to take delivery of a new van. On the way home along the motorway the driver heard a loud noise as he pulled back into the nearside lane. Looking into his outside mirror he saw a large wheel strike a Mini which was about to overtake him. He pulled onto the hard shoulder to help clear the road and found that the wheel was from his van. The wheel carrier beneath the rear of the body had come adrift and allowed the wheel to fall off into the path of the Mini causing extensive damage to it.

The claim from the Mini driver was dealt with by the insurers of the van coachbuilders as a public liability claim. The refitting of the wheel carrier was not included in the claim.

Policies normally exclude liability arising from the use of motor vehicles (these can be insured under a motor insurance) and aircraft or watercraft (insurable in the aviation and marine departments).

Policies may also exclude liability for defective products which can be insured under a product liability insurance. Separate policies are available in respect of professional negligence.

Although all traders require insurances indemnifying them in respect of their liability to others, different types of policy are necessary for different risks. The type of insurance required by a shopkeeper differs from that needed by a factory owner. Builders and decorators, window cleaners, and garage proprietors all have different liability problems and require different cover. Supermarkets and restaurants also need different policies.

Claims in respect of food served in a restaurant would be dealt with under a public liability insurance, whereas claims in respect of food purchased and taken away to be eaten fall under product liability.

Product liability

All those who sell goods incur a legal liability to others in respect of personal injury, death or illness, or any other loss or damage that may arise. This liability exists whether the goods are for sale in the United Kingdom or abroad. In fact, the problems of claims from overseas countries involve a need for knowledge of the laws of those countries and, preferably, facilities for dealing with claims in them. Where exporting to North America is likely, premiums will be much higher than for other areas.

Product liability risks are excluded from most public liability insurances as insurers prefer to deal with them by the issue of a separate policy.

The person selling the goods has the primary liability and would need to defend an action. If he or she is not also the manufacturer he or she can bring that person, or anyone else involved, into the action. In some cases many defendants are involved. One example of this situation was a case of dermatitis following the wearing of a new fur coat. Investigation revealed that after the skins had been obtained from the animal various specialists washed, treated, coloured and prepared them before they were tailored into a garment. All these people, together with the tailor and the retailer, were defendants in the subsequent action.

Example

The publican stood a fresh crate of lemonade on a shelf behind
the bar. As he pulled the first bottle the neck broke in his hand
severing an artery. His claim against the lemonade manufacturer was rejected on the grounds that the fault was in the
bottle. The bottle-makers examined the glass and claimed that
it was up to their usual standard. Further investigations
revealed that the makers of the crate had reduced the size of
the compartments by a few millimetres, sufficient to retain the
hold on the bottle for longer than previously experienced. This
had caused the publican to put excessive strain on the neck of
the bottle in order to withdraw it from the crate.

In the subsequent court action the main liability fell on the
crate makers.

There are many more examples:
  (a) mistakes made in the preparation of food or foodstuffs for ani-
      mals can be the subject of a claim;
  (b) harmful materials used in make-up or in hairstyling can cause
      adverse reactions;
  (c) fireworks exploding prematurely;
  (d) gas or other chemicals escaping from the containers in which
      they are stored;
  (e) faulty materials used in the manufacture of tools.

Some insurers are prepared to consider insurances in which the
proposer makes it clear that he or she would wish to have a product
liability claim settled even if the third party could not prove the loss.
An example would be a case in which a propeller came off a shaft
damaging a test bed. Although the claimant could not prove that the
damage caused was the fault of the manufacturer, the manufacturer
felt that it was "commercially" desirable that the customer be reimbursed. Obviously a higher premium would be charged and the
insured required to assume part of the loss (an excess) or actually
share the loss.

There are instances in which the insurer may well consider that
what is being asked for is not product insurance but some form of
product guarantee. An example would be failure of anti-corrosive
paint causing the need for the removal of all the paint and cleaning

of the surface, followed by prepainting and repainting with fresh anti-corrosive paint. This clearly is not a case where there is a claim for bodily injury or loss or damage to property. However, unless the insurer excludes this type of claim he or she might well be prepared to accept it and charge a premium accordingly. Obviously the types of risk vary so much that where manufacturing is involved underwriting is on an individual basis.

Unless it is specifically excluded, most insurers are prepared to accept claims arising from defects in design as product liability. These must result in loss or damage and not, in fact, be the result of professional negligence (which is insurable elsewhere).

Retailers cannot insert clauses protecting themselves in respect of claims from the public. They are prevented from doing so by the Sale of Goods Act 1979. They can, of course, recover losses due to defects from the manufacturer or importer unless there are restrictions imposed in the supply agreement. The existence of the Consumer Protection Act 1987 now makes it more difficult for manufacturers to escape liability. Retailers can bring the manufacturers into an action as co-defendants. The retailer will still require product liability insurance in order to meet the costs of defending an action.

The Consumer Protection Act 1987 states that if a product is defective the producer or importer is liable for any damage caused. If the supplier cannot identify the manufacturer or importer then he or she will be liable. To be defective the goods must be below the standard one expects to find. At the present moment it will be a good enough defence for a manufacturer to claim that at the time of manufacture existing knowledge was such that it was not possible to realise that there was a defect in the goods.

In a nutshell the Act does not require anyone hurt by a defective product to prove negligence against its producer to recover compensation. Where the possibility exists that some of the product is likely to be defective manufacturers endeavour to recall the product. This introduces a complex process of seeking out the product and having as many units as possible returned to the factory. Insurance is available against this possibility but it is difficult to obtain more than part insurance.

As the Act is concerned with "consumers" it is not intended to apply other than to damage sustained by property that is for private use, occupation or consumption. However the "strict" element is thought to apply to all goods and not be restricted by the title of the Act.

Professional indemnity

This too is a class of risk not covered under the public liability insurance. Liability arises from the professional person giving negligent advice which results in loss. In the past liability has arisen irrespective of the fact that a fee has not been charged for the advice given.

The range of those who claim to be professionals and who offer advice or provide a specialist service is very great. A few examples are given below:

(a) *Doctors* Until the late 1980s the field was limited to one major insurer who provided cover at a fixed premium. We are now witnessing a situation in which the extent of liability between the general practitioner and the consultant is resulting in the setting up of flexible premium rates. More companies are now entering the market and changes are apparent. The claims possible vary from negligent advice to unsuccessful surgical operations.

(b) *Surveyors* A great deal of money can be lost if a surveyor has been negligent in surveying a property.

(c) *Accountants* The result of an audit or the provision of final accounts can be the basis on which major business decisions are taken. An error due to negligence could cause financial ruin to a client.

(d) A *pharmacist* could make an error in completing a prescription with harmful results to his or her customer.

(e) An *insurance broker* who overlooks the issue of a cover note could be responsible for a substantial loss if the insurers were to refuse an indemnity.

Personal liability

Everyone owes a duty to others not to cause them injury nor to cause damage to their property. Liability under this heading relates to liability as private citizens. All other liability, such as that which relates to a trade, business or profession or in connection with the ownership or use of vehicles or property is excluded.

In a private capacity people engage in sport, own animals or bicycles — whatever one does in day to day life involves some liability.

Policies are usually issued in respect of all members of the insured's family resident with him or her (children away at boarding school or university are treated as "resident with him or her").

Liability cover is not unlimited but may be as high as £1M. Cover is not restricted to the insured's home but applies anywhere in the United Kingdom. Many insurers extend cover during temporary visits abroad.

Example

William came out of the shop, waved his hand to the friendly shopkeeper and walked out into the road. A squealing of brakes drew his attention to a motorcycle just a few feet away from him. Simultaneously the motorcycle swerved and hit a lamppost. To William's horror the rider fell from the machine with blood streaming from his face.

The motorcyclist sued William for negligence and was awarded substantial damages in respect of his injuries.

Occupier's liability

As an occupier one has a liability to any person who may be invited onto the premises or suffer injury as a result of the occupier's negligence. There are also certain liabilities an occupier has towards trespassers. The primary liability rests with the occupier even if he or she is not also the owner. Liability for defects in the building which may cause injury (such as loose tiles) can only be deflected to the owner if he or she has been informed and, within a reasonable time, has failed to take the necessary action.

Claims made against the householder by members of his or her family resident with him or her would also be excluded.

Example

Jill felt sorry for her neighbour Mrs Jones who was in bed

suffering from influenza and so she went to visit her. She opened the door and stepping into the hall called up the stairs "It's me, Jill. Can I come up?" Her grateful neighbour called back "Yes. Please do". Jill went slowly up the stairs but just before she reached the top the heel of her shoe caught in a hole in the stair carpet. She slipped and fell injuring her left leg.

Using the hall telephone she called a taxi and went to the private clinic in the town where she was found to have a fracture.

Subsequently she sued her neighbours, Mr and Mrs Jones, for negligence (and also cited the Occupiers' Liability Act 1957) and was awarded damages and costs.

Property owner's liability

A property owner could be liable for injury caused to third parties as a result of lack of maintenance of his or her property. This would exclude injury to employees which can be covered under an employers' liability insurance.

To cater for the requirements of the Defective Premises Act 1972, cover under the policy is extended to any building owned by the policyholder during the previous seven years.

Policies are also extended to cover the liability of a purchaser who has signed a contract to purchase the property. The extension would not apply if the purchaser has arranged his or her own insurance on the building.

Legal expenses insurance

Although not strictly liability insurance, it is expedient to consider legal expenses insurance at this point. It is a very new type of insurance and is intended to provide the legal expenses necessary to defend or initiate a legal action.

The situations which can arise are many and include actions brought by customers, employees or neighbours. As has been shown many claims against a policyholder may be dealt with by existing liability insurances. However, situations may arise in which an indemnity is not granted by an insurance policy. In addition, the insured may need to take legal action to protect his or her interests and the existence of the insurance would enable this to be done without using or earmarking his or her own capital.

The importance of good legal advice and the best possible legal representation in a court cannot be over estimated.

There are very many statutes affecting traders, as the list below illustrates:

Race Relations Act 1976
Sex Discrimination Act 1976
Health and Safety At Work, etc Act 1974
Trade Descriptions Acts, 1968 and 1972
Acts relating to taxes and VAT

Examples are:
(a) an action by a customer alleging defective goods would not fall to be dealt with by a product liability insurance if no injury or loss is alleged;
(b) an employee referring a dispute to an industrial tribunal;
(c) a prosecution under the Weights and Measures Acts;
(d) the need to seek an injunction against a neighbour whose development is likely to have an adverse effect on customers visiting the premises;
(e) an action against an individual assaulting you or one of your staff;
(f) a dispute with a supplier of goods.

Fidelity guarantee insurance

Basically, the object of this class of insurance is to indemnify an employer against financial loss caused by the dishonesty of employees. The employer's money may be handled by cashiers, representatives, shop managers, rent collectors, insurance agents, shop assistants and many other employees.

The policy indemnifies the insured in respect of money or stock misappropriated by employees. Insurance may be obtained in respect of individual employees or a collective insurance would name those employees concerned and the limit of indemnity in respect of each. Changes of staff would need to be notified to insurers immediately.

Much more usual today are policies covering a group of employees or the entire staff for one overall sum. As a single amount "floats" over the whole group the policies are called "floating" insurances. All losses discovered during the insurance, and for 18 to 24 months afterwards (so long as they took place during the period of insurance), are covered.

In fidelity guarantee insurance employers complete the usual proposal form but must also submit a detailed form (known as an "applicant's form") completed by each person who is to be guaranteed. This form will provide details of the individual's status (married or single), his or her dependants, whether he or she owns his or her own home, salary and previous employment, his or her financial position (that is such things as debts, bankruptcy and the ownership of life insurance).

In addition, they will make extensive enquiries to establish how the employer selects staff and what sort of references are required and how they are checked. Except for large employers, insurers prefer to investigate new employees on behalf of employers and will charge a small fee for the work.

If a loss is proved against an employee, proceedings will be taken to recover the loss.

Engineering insurance

Insurance is available in respect of breakdown of most types of machinery including computers. Insurance is also available in respect of steam boilers and pressure plant.

Many items of equipment, including lifts and lifting machinery, cranes, steam boilers, air and steam pressure vessels must be regularly inspected by law and a certificate completed by a "competent person". The insurance provides cover against damage caused to the plant from an external source or from its own breakdown.

Insurers are able to provide an inspection service and their qualified engineers can sign the necessary certification. The types of equipment which must be inspected regularly and certified are increasing and many appliances formerly excluded now fall within the regulations.

In addition, insurers provide an indemnity in respect of damage to other plant belonging to the insured or a third party and for personal injury.

Losses resulting from business interruption following a breakdown can also be covered.

Credit insurance

This class of insurance is to protect businesses from losses which may result if a buyer defaults or becomes insolvent or bankrupt. Cover is never offered on a 100% indemnity basis and the insured is always liable to share the loss in an agreed proportion. There are two reasons for this. One is to remove the possibility of insuring profits (so the insurers only become liable for the invoice price). Secondly, insurers feel that if the insured is a co-insurer for an amount, however small, he or she will have an interest in clearing or reducing the loss.

Businesses may insure selected accounts on the possibility that those particular firms may fail to pay for one of the reasons mentioned. A lower rate per cent will be quoted for those businesses that insure their entire credit risk. The number and size of accounts and period of credit will affect the premium charged.

Overseas business is not covered by commercial insurers but is dealt with by the Export Credit Guarantee Department of the DTI.

Motor insurance

Since 1930 it has been compulsory in the United Kingdom to insure in respect of third party claims resulting in personal injury or death. Originally only restricted to third parties not travelling in the vehicle it was later extended to all third parties and to conform with European Community law has been extended to cover third party property damage.

The Road Traffic Acts require an unlimited indemnity in respect of personal injury but, in the case of property damage, it may be restricted to £67,000. In practice motor third party insurance provides unlimited cover except in the insurance of commercial vehicles where there are upper limits.

There are two main forms of cover available:

(a) *Third party only*

This allows the insured to drive a car on a road in compliance with the Road Traffic Acts. Insurers pay for personal injury to third parties, including passengers, and for third party property (including third party cars) damaged in an accident. Insurers pay for emergency treatment given by a doctor following an accident and also for hospital treatment of third party claimants who succeed in their claim against an insured.

In order that they may be able to fully control third party claims, insurers pay the solicitor's fees for representation at a coroner's inquest or in a magistrates' court if a third party claim is possible. In practice, insurers may feel it necessary to defend the insured in any court if a substantial third party claim is involved.

The legal liability of passengers is also included (for example a passenger may open a car door and strike a passing cyclist).

For a small extra premium based on the value of the vehicle insurers will include cover for fire and/or theft of the vehicle. Theft cover includes damage that has been caused to a vehicle that is stolen and later recovered.

(b) *Comprehensive*

In addition to the cover granted by the third party policy, fire and theft cover is included. Damage or the loss of the vehicle from other causes is also insured. The comprehensive policy includes a number of additional benefits such as accident insurance for the insured and spouse (a substantial lump sum for death or serious injury), medical expenses for the driver and all passengers (usually £200 per person) and a cover for personal effects (usually £100).

The most important advantage of the comprehensive insurance over the third party policy is the fact that following an accident the insured can have repairs put in hand without using his or her own capital to pay for the damage. Even if the fault is not the driver's own there are the costs and difficulties in recovering from the other party. How many people return to the car park to find their car dented? Apart from the doubtful liability of the car park operator from whom do we seek recompense in the absence of comprehensive insurance?

Most insurers allow the insured to instruct repairs where

damage is small but will require to be able to inspect the vehicle at the repairers in the case of more serious damage.

Replacement of window glass and windscreens, although included in the policy wording of "the vehicle", is usually treated separately so as not to affect the "no claim discount". The reason is purely a competitive one, but recently insurers have begun to impose excesses due to the volume and costs of the claims experienced.

Accessories and spare parts are also insured if they are on the vehicle or in the insured's private garage.

Competition is still high for desirable risks which are family cars used by mature drivers with good records. A variety of free benefits are offered to encourage these owners to transfer their car insurances.

The insured is usually able to reduce his or her premium by accepting some liability in respect of loss or damage to the vehicle. In some cases insurers impose such excesses compulsorily. Sometimes it is because special schemes are being offered but it may also be related to the age and experience of the drivers concerned or because of the poor record of particular drivers.

In the case of commercial vehicles, the third party section of the policy indemnifies the insured in respect of injury to third parties during the loading and unloading of the vehicle.

The insured, under a private motor policy that is not in the name of a firm, is usually granted cover for third party only whilst driving another vehicle not belonging to him or her. This does not extend to cover the vehicle being driven. Insurance policies allow driving of the insured vehicle by any one authorised by the insured. Discounts are normally available if driving is restricted to the insured or a named driver (in many cases "insured and spouse" driving restriction).

Insurers are required by the Road Traffic Acts to issue a certificate of insurance to policyholders. The certificate is evidence of the existence of cover under that Act. In effect the holder is allowed by law to use the vehicle on a road. Until fairly recently certificates showed the registration details of the insured vehicles. It is now more usual to state that cover is granted in respect of any vehicle owned by the insured (or being purchased by him or her by hire purchase). Most insurers insist on being advised of a change of vehicle within 14 days of commencing to use it. Failure to do so would not affect the cover required by law, but it would invalidate the remainder of the policy cover.

Temporary certificates are issued at inception of the insurance until the permanent certificate of insurance has been printed and issued. Certificates are also attached to a renewal notice covering the insured for a period (usually 14 or 15 days) after the insurance has expired. The cover is not related to renewal of the insurance or otherwise but ceases if another insurer issues cover.

Cover, either in the form of a certificate of insurance or a cover note, must not be back dated. It is an offence to drive a vehicle unless there is a certificate of insurance in force in relation to the driving of that vehicle.

Although the policy covers use within the European Community such cover is restricted to that required by law in the country concerned. It is, therefore, advisable to arrange in advance with insurers to provide the full policy cover whilst the vehicle is abroad. An international motor insurance card (known as a "green card") is issued showing the countries to be visited. An endorsement is also issued extending the policy cover to the countries concerned. Policy cover includes loading or unloading the vehicle at an airport or seaport, including the transit risk. Some insurers do not charge if the visit is for a period under one month to a west European country.

The green card, as it has become known over the years, is accepted in most countries outside the European Community. The list does vary from time to time and anyone travelling outside the EC should check before travelling. At the present time it is accepted in:

Bulgaria, Greece (although a member of the EC, this country requires a green card to be produced), Iceland, Israel, Iran, Iraq, Malta, Morocco, Poland, Rumania, Tunisia, Turkey and Yugoslavia.

In the absence of a green card it will be necessary to buy local insurance at short term rates.

The no claim discount is peculiar to motor insurance and barely exists in any other class of insurance. It is a discount from the premium allowed at renewal for an insured who has been free of claims in the previous year. In order to encourage a reduction in claims, insurers offer a progressive scale as the insured remains free of claims. This system, however, results in a great deal of controversy. Insureds have to realise that it is not a "no blame" discount. It depends on an additional factor — recovery of the insurer's loss.

To be "free of claims" means not to have an accident which is the fault of the driver of the policyholder's vehicle. In addition it must be possible for insurers to recover their loss from the third party. As most insurers have "knock for knock" agreements with each other, action is not undertaken for recovery of losses. By virtue of the agreement each insurer pays for repairs to his or her insured's vehicle (if cover is comprehensive). Each insurer decides on the facts available to him or her. If it is believed that the policyholder, or the authorised driver at the time of the accident, is free of blame the discount is not lost. If, however, the other driver cannot be traced, or has no insurance and cannot pay, the no claim discount is lost.

One reliable way of saving the no claim discount exists if there is an excess on the insured's policy or if there are any uninsured losses (for example, personal injury). The insured (generally using a solicitor or one of the motoring organisations) who has recovered the excess or been successful in recovering the loss from the third party or third party insurers can claim that in the absence of insurance he or she could have recovered the entire loss. Thus there is an entitlement to the "no claim discount". Most insurers, on receiving proof, will be prepared to confirm that the no claim discount is not affected by that incident.

Example

Mr Brown was driving in a stream of traffic which was thickening as it neared an area in which road repairs were taking place. Just before reaching the road works a motorcycle veered towards him and, before he could take avoiding action, it had hit his car throwing the rider over his bonnet. Whilst the injured motorcyclist was being put into the ambulance Mr Brown found a witness to the accident — the driver of the car in front of his.

Mr Brown's insurers paid for repairs to the car, excluding his £50 excess. He successfully claimed against the motorcyclist's insurers for the £50 and the cost of hiring a car for three days whilst repairs were in progress. Mr Brown sent proof to his own insurers who wrote to him confirming that his "no claim discount" was unaffected by the incident.

A no claim discount is not affected by a claim for windscreen or glass damage including consequent scratching of paintwork. Nor is it affected by a claim for emergency treatment.

Many insurers offer schemes to protect the no claim discount. The "guaranteed" discount means that insurers will automatically allow the discount earned irrespective of claims reported. This type of contract is offered to older drivers and may involve slightly higher premiums and an excess. Another scheme uses the term "protected" discount. An example of this is where insurers state that two claims in a period of three years will not invalidate the discount.

The discount is progressive on a scale, generally from 30% to 60% of the premium to be paid. In the case of commercial vehicle policies the percentage allowed is much less.

If there is more than one vehicle on a policy schedule each earns its own discount separately. Where there are many vehicles owned by the same company or group, special terms, referred to as "fleet" rates, are offered. The premium for the fleet would be based entirely on the claims experienced by that fleet.

If someone in the employ of the policyholder suffers injury arising from the use of the vehicle in the course of that employment no indemnity is provided. A claim in these circumstances would be covered by an employers' liability insurance.

Who may drive the vehicle and the use to which it may be put will depend on the type of motor insurance policy and the conditions of use. The cheapest cover relates to "social, domestic and pleasure" which involves no business use of any description. The most expensive types are for cars used by representatives and commercial vehicles used by long distance haulage contractors.

Travel insurance

Previously titled "baggage" insurance this type of cover was offered piecemeal. Insurers would offer insurance of the traveller's personal effects, personal accident and medical expenses with a form of cancellation cover. The proposer would select the sum insured in each case. As the variety of items of cover increased insurers offered discounts to proposers who selected a number of items of cover together.

Most insurers today offer a package that includes luggage (and personal effects), money carried, medical expenses outside the United

Kingdom, costs of hospital treatment, losses due to cancellation (caused by unavoidable situations), personal accident insurance (with special schemes for winter sports) and legal liability to others. The sums insured are usually standardised. One proposal form is normally provided and, in many cases, brokers and travel agents are authorised to issue policies on behalf of insurers.

This results in a very keen and competitive market. It is also a very necessary form of cover, often neglected by travellers; more and more tour operators and travel agents are endeavouring to include cover in the holiday package on offer unless the prospective traveller objects.

Rates quoted are usually based on three separate areas:

(a) United Kingdom only;
(b) Europe (generally including countries not in Europe but bordering the Mediterranean, and Jordan) as defined in the literature;
(c) world-wide.

Some insurers do not offer policies restricted to the United Kingdom only and others issue cover for USA and Canada separately.

The period of cover can be as short as four or five days, in some cases, to 31 days. Extra periods may sometimes be added, although insurers may have a maximum of six months.

Reduced premiums may be offered to children under, say, 12 years of age with free cover for younger children. Premiums may be doubled for those over 60 seeking world-wide cover. Extra premiums are quoted for hazardous activities, such as winter sports.

Family policies, offering a special premium for a husband and wife and up to four children are also available.

Policy cover

(a) *Luggage (or baggage)*

Policy cover is in respect of loss or damage to luggage and clothes being worn or carried. This is described as all risks cover and is subject to the restrictions mentioned when describing all risks cover earlier. The sum insured varies from insurer to insurer but will be between £1000 and £1500. There may be separate limits in respect of certain items, such as jewellery or cameras, and a single item limit. Most travellers do not consider the value of the effects that they take with them. Certainly a family travelling to a European holiday resort for two weeks will find the cover sufficient. A family going on a world cruise may need more cover.

It is general practice to impose an excess, usually about £25, to avoid having to deal with small claims.

Most policies are now extended to allow for a payment to cover temporary items in the event of the baggage being lost for over 12 hours. The sum is quite small, usually about £50, and caters for emergency clothing and toiletries.

(b) *Personal accident*

The cover here is in respect of capital sums (that is, excluding weekly benefits for temporary disablement) following the loss of limbs, permanent disablement or death. The sums involved are in the range of £15,000 to £25,000. The holders of credit cards and charge cards are given free cover ranging from £25,000 to £100,000 if the flight, tour or holiday booking is paid for by using the card.

(c) *Cancellation*

The object of this very important section is to provide cover in respect of payments made for a holiday which has to be cancelled for any of a number of reasons. They include death, accident or illness which affects the insured, spouse (sometimes includes other relatives), a close business associate or a member of the party travelling with the insured. Included too is the quarantine of the insured person, jury service or witness duty, redundancy, pregnancy, burglary, fire or flood at the insured's home. Insurance policies vary in respect of many of the last named hazards and there is usually an excess of about £25 applicable.

Additional cover may also be given which includes delays in departure in excess of 24 hours due to bad weather, industrial action or breakdown affecting the ship or aircraft.

Curtailment of a holiday due to any of the reasons listed for cancellation may be included in this section of the policy or as a separate item. This means that the costs of rearranging a holiday will be met. Some policies provide for compensation based on the loss of days as a percentage of the holiday costs.

(d) *Medical expenses*

The cost of medical treatment outside the United Kingdom is

the main component of this section and the maximum cover per person may be as high as £½M. Certainly this sum is essential in many areas, such as the USA. To avoid payment for minor ailments an excess of £25 usually applies. Most insurers do not request details of the proposer's medical condition but would not wish to cover anyone travelling against doctor's orders or for medical treatment overseas. Routine treatment of a pre-existing condition may also be excluded.

Medical expenses generally include medical and surgical fees, hospital, nursing home, massage and dental fees. The additional hotel and travelling expenses of other members of the party affected by the situation are also included together with the costs of a nurse to travel back to the United Kingdom with the insured if necessary.

Reciprocal medical arrangements exist in EC Member States and in some other countries and details should be obtained from the DSS before travelling. Generally only a partial medical service is offered.

Emergency assistance is a new and developing feature of travel insurance. The cover offered by these schemes can be obtained by individuals but is increasingly being bought by insurers offering travel policies. Most of them have a 24 hour hot-line with multi-lingual staff available. They will guarantee or make local arrangements for payment of doctors' and hospital bills, arrange for immediate transfer for medical treatment or repatriation. The decision is taken based on their medical consultant's knowledge of local facilities and the specific medical condition of the insured. Air ambulances are also available in some cases. Those marketing the scheme claim that immediate treatment often depends on guarantees being given in the local language.

(e) *Personal liability*
Cover up to £1M is given in respect of the insured's legal liability for injury to others or damage to their property.

(f) *Delayed departure*
Some policies provide a payment if departure is delayed due to bad weather, industrial action or breakdown. The amounts and

times vary but a reasonable guide would be £60 for 24 hours'
delay. There are insurers offering payment for 12 hours' delay
with an additional payment for each 12 hours up to a maximum
of £60.

Most policies now provide for missed departures due to failure
of public transport to arrive on time. Similar cover may be given
for return departure. It is anticipated that this type of cover may
shortly be extended, by some insurers, to apply to all transport
failures.

Many insurers also offer additional items of cover, for example
hijack, loss of passport, failure of tour organiser or withdrawal of
service (such as waiters at the holiday hotel).

For those travelling regularly throughout the year an annual policy
is very much cheaper to buy.

Personal accident insurance

Personal accident insurance is intended to provide benefits to a claimant who has suffered serious injury or death following an accident or
who is unable to work for a period of time as a result of an accident.

It is available to individuals or on a group basis. Group schemes are
bought by clubs for their members and are attractive to sports clubs,
or may be purchased by employers, who may or may not obtain
contributions from employees.

Benefits are divided between "capital" sums — that is lump sum
payments for death, permanent disablement and loss of limbs or sight.
Weekly benefits are paid for temporary total disablement or temporary
partial disablement at a lower rate. The usual explanation of temporary
total disablement is "unable to follow his or her usual occupation" but
the policy could define it as "unable to follow any occupation". The
difference is crucial.

The schedule of a personal accident insurance policy will generally
list the benefits available as follows:

Death or
Loss of both arms or an arm and a leg or   }   the sum of
Permanent loss of sight or   £10,000
Permanent total disablement

Loss of a leg or an arm   the sum of £5000

Medical expenses   (up to 15% of above sums)

Temporary total disablement   £100 p.w.

Temporary partial disablement   £40 p.w.

Increased benefits are available but insurers try to restrict the weekly benefits to 75% of an insured's average earnings.

The loss must arise from an accident and not from sickness or disease. However, if the sickness or disease follows naturally from the accident it would be an acceptable claim under the insurance.

Example

Charles was caught in a storm while out riding his motorcycle one evening. The wind caught him as he turned a corner and he hit a tree. He fell into a ditch full of water and found that he could not move. He was unconscious when they found him in the morning. He was taken to hospital where he was found to have multiple fractures and a severe cold. The cold developed into pneumonia from which he died.

The claim for "death following an accident" was accepted under his personal accident insurance.

The case of Arthur was very different as there was no "natural" relationship between the accident and his death. There was a fresh set of circumstances intervening: the patient in the next bed who had diphtheria.

Example

Arthur was out riding his horse when he was thrown to the ground breaking his leg. He was taken to hospital. The patient in the next bed became ill and was found to have diphtheria. Subsequently Arthur also contracted diphtheria from which he died.

Insurers refused an indemnity under his personal accident insurance.

Premiums are based mainly on occupation and, for this purpose, insurers group occupations. Additional hazards in the occupation or pursuit (such as pot-holing) affect the group in which a proposed insurance will be placed.

Insurers will want to know about the insured's occupation and what he or she actually does. If he is a woodworker, does he use machinery? If he is a builder, up to what heights does he work? There is an exclusion of suicide which is usually only applied if positive proof exists.

For rating purposes there is a division into four classes:

Class 1. Professional administrative and clerical.

Class 2. Skilled with moderate manual work or semi-skilled with a small amount of manual work.

Class 3. Skilled but predominantly manual or semi-skilled with moderate manual work.

Class 4. Semi-skilled, mainly manual or physically strenuous work.

Cover for disease and sickness may be added. This would be in the form of a weekly payment for temporary total disablement although permanent disablement following an illness may also be available.

So far as the sickness benefit is concerned insurers are conscious of the fact that most people are sick for short periods every year. In order to avoid small claims they will impose an excess or a franchise. A franchise is used more frequently and in practice it means that an insurer will not pay for a claim that is below the franchise but will pay in full if it is over (different to an excess which is always deducted). Thus if a seven day franchise is imposed an insured sick for seven days or less cannot claim but an insured sick for eight or more days receives settlement of his or her claim in full.

The continental scale of benefits may be used by some insurers. In this system the policy schedule states a capital sum. A percentage of that sum being paid in respect of the type of disablement. Proposers are asked to state if they are right or left handed. Some examples, from the schedule are listed below:

Loss of both hands	100%
Loss of both feet	100%
Loss of right arm or hand	60%
Loss of left arm or hand	60%

Loss of thumb of right hand	20%
Loss of index finger of left hand	10%
Complete and irrecoverable loss of hearing in one ear	10%
Loss of big toe	5%

Policies are available in which cover is restricted to accidental death only or for accidental death, loss of limbs or total disablement following an accident. It is also possible to insure for weekly benefits only (which could be used to pay for medical expenses following an accident).

Group schemes are available for employees but, unless the workforce is substantial, individual proposal forms will be sought. The benefits are usually related to earnings. As an example the scale of benefits could be:

death, loss of limbs or sight or permanent total disablement	three year's salary
temporary total disablement	half of weekly earnings (employees would also claim the State sickness benefit).

The policy is issued in the employer's name and payments made to the employer. The employer may obtain contributions from employees or pay the premiums himself or herself. Insurers are not affected by these arrangements. Employers may wish to use this type of policy and DSS benefits in order to pay employees who are absent from work following an accident or sickness their full salary for a given period.

In cases in which policies are issued to clubs and other similar organisations, the benefits are paid to the policyholder and not directly to the member.

Life insurance

Although there are only a few different types of insurance in existence they are packaged in a variety of ways by the many life insurers. In addition they carry brand names accorded to them by marketing departments which make it difficult for ordinary mortals to compare their relative values. At the present time the law affecting the selling of life insurance is controlled by the Financial Services Act 1986 which came into force in January 1988.

Life insurance may be obtained from life insurance companies and societies and insurance intermediaries in the same way as other classes of insurance, although it has to be said that it is usually "sold" to, rather than sought by, the public. As a protection against pressure selling, insurers are required to send a notice to the insured allowing 14 days in which the insurance can be cancelled and any premium already paid will be refunded. Some insurers have extended this period voluntarily to 30 days.

Most insurers now require proposers to sign a medical consent form so that if it is decided to apply to the proposer's GP for a medical report they will not have to contact the proposer again. Medical information is excluded from the Data Protection Act but the Access to Medical Reports Act 1988 gives a right for a patient to see a report before it is sent to insurers. Insurers will give the proposer 21 days to contact the doctor and arrange to see the report. If the proposer fails to do so the doctor will then send it to insurers. If the proposer wishes he or she may apply to the doctor within six months to see the report. There may be a charge for providing a copy.

A doctor can, in certain circumstances, refuse access to the report or part of it. If he or she reveals only part of the report the patient must be told this.

There is also industrial life insurance (now more usually referred to as "home service insurance") which is sold by representatives of those insurers transacting it. The representatives collect premiums weekly, fortnightly or annually from the homes of the premium payers and also settle claims that arise. Fewer types of insurance are transacted and the premiums and sums insured are smaller than in ordinary life insurance. Strict Government regulations have existed over many years to protect those who find the need to pay their premiums in this way.

In most cases it is possible to obtain insurance by payment of a lump sum rather than an annual premium. Some insurers specialise in offering a range of "bonds" designed for those with large sums to invest.

The basic types of life insurance policy and their particular uses are listed below.

Term insurance

This is the original type of life insurance policy available. It simply is an agreement by a life insurer to pay a certain sum of money on the death of the life insured during the term of the insurance. Originally these policies were issued on an annual basis to adults under 45 years of age. The insured would need to be fit to be able to obtain a fresh insurance at the end of the year. At the present time policies may be effected for very short periods (perhaps a week to cover a special contingency, such as a business trip to a troubled area) or for, say, five or ten years.

They do have a use for a young married person needing maximum life insurance at minimum premium. Insurers issue term insurances that may be converted, without further proof of health, to whole life or endowment insurances during the term.

If the policy is discontinued by the premium payer there is no return of any premiums paid.

A very popular form of term insurance is the "decreasing term insurance". This is usually advertised as a mortgage protection policy. The insurance is effected for a similar sum to that borrowed under the repayment mortgage and the sum insured reduces annually. At the same time the life insured is getting older and would expect to pay more premium. It can be seen that one action (annual reduction of sum insured) counter balances the other (increase of age) so that the premium is kept constant throughout the term of the insurance. In the event of the death of the life insured during the term of the insurance the mortgage debt is repaid by the insurers. Once again there is no refund of premiums in the event of cancellation by the insured.

Another form of term insurance is the "family income insurance". This is similar to a decreasing term insurance except that it pays an income to a dependant. Any sum agreed to be paid annually is paid from the date of death to the expiry of the term. There are policies that pay an increasing sum each year to allow for inflation. These are, of course, more costly.

Example

Giles effected a family income policy which would pay his dependants £10,000 a year for 20 years. He died soon after completing the insurance. His dependants received 20 payments of £10,000 = £200,000.

Martin effected a similar insurance and died 15 years later. His dependants received only five payments of £10,000 = £50,000.

It is also possible to obtain joint insurances that commence payment after the first death. In the modern world there could be the same financial difficulties whichever partner died first, so that such insurances are becoming more popular.

The various forms of term insurance are the very cheapest form of life insurance available. At the present time, due to the AIDS statistics, many insurers quote heavily increased premiums in respect of young male age groups. A very few have excluded death from AIDS or AIDS related disease.

Some insurers' tables are for non-smokers with increased premiums for smokers. Others may be for smokers with a discount for non-smokers.

If the policy is designed to be sold with a personal pension plan an insured who is self-employed may be able to obtain tax relief on the premiums paid.

Whole life insurance

These policies are designed to provide a cash sum at the death of the life insured at any time. Premiums may be paid throughout life or calculated to cease at an agreed age (for example at retirement). If the insured cancels the policy after two or three years a surrender value is available. Alternatives are to borrow cash on the security of the policy from the insurers or a bank. It is also possible to obtain a fully paid up policy for that proportion of the original policy actually bought.

This type of insurance is used as a protection for dependants. The sum insured under the basic policy may be enhanced by payment of a small additional premium which arises from sharing in the profit made by the insurer. Fairly new to life insurance is the "unit linked" life insurance policies. The difference is that the premiums, after payment for the life insurance benefit, are invested in separate funds (most insurers have a choice of funds and also allow transfer between funds).

The fund may be invested in particular shares (examples are property, oil, Government stock, Japan, USA, gold). Since the stock markets took a tumble late in 1987, and insureds found that shares can go down as well as up, a few insurers have issued policies in which the premiums are shared between the two methods. Profit sharing is the more stable method but the unit linked portion has possibilities of higher growth.

A possible use for these insurances is to provide capital to allow partners to buy the shares of a deceased partner after his or her death. In many cases this could prevent failure of the business due to withdrawal of capital by the family of the deceased.

It is also possible to insure the life of a key employee whose unexpec-ted demise would seriously affect the profitability of the business. This type of insurance, known as "key person" insurance is to provide the employer with a sum to cover the costs involved in replacing and training a replacement, as well as any losses of business arising in the process. It can be paid to employers in instalments over an agreed period of time. Premiums are treated as a business expense and pay-ments by insurers as taxable income of the business.

Group life insurance may be obtained by employers and is usually, but not necessarily, associated with a group pension scheme. Cover is normally against death in-service and is expressed as a relationship with salary (possibly four times annual salary). Group life insurance is usually a benefit given by the employer. Premiums are based on the total salary bill and are adjusted annually.

Endowment insurance

These are the most popular of the life insurance policies. In return for the premium paid insurers will provide a lump sum at the end of an agreed period of years or at death if this is earlier. The longer the period of years selected, the larger the sum obtainable for a given premium. In addition, insureds may effect policies on a profit sharing basis ("with profits") or have them unit-linked.

As in the case of whole life insurances there are surrender values, loans and fully paid up policies available if required.

Policies effected for the exclusive benefit of a wife and/or children can be protected from creditors by being placed in trust under the Married Women's Property Act 1882.

The endowment insurance is extensively used at the present time for house purchase. Building societies lending money against the security of a property under a repayment mortgage calculate repayments over the period of the mortgage granted so that each represents part repayment of the capital sum and part repayment of the interest on the loan. As the outstanding debt to the building society reduces, the interest paid also gets smaller. If a property is purchased using an endowment insurance, the interest remains constant over the whole term of the loan and is repaid when the endowment matures.

Example

Tom Smith asked the local building society to quote for an endowment mortgage for the house he wished to buy. The quotation was as follows:

Interest at 12½% on loan of £60,000 for 25 years = £7500 per annum (actual monthly payment would include a tax rebate in respect of interest on the first £30,000).

Assuming that Tom paid the standard rate of tax, they quoted a monthly net interest of £546.88.

The endowment insurance premium which he would pay throughout the period was quoted as £130 per month, making a total of £676.88 per month. If the endowment insurance was effected on a profits basis the accumulated profits would accrue to his benefit.

A "low cost" scheme was also suggested. In this case the society quoted for a smaller endowment than £60,000 on a profits basis. This sum, they explained, would be increased by the profits as they accumulated and after repayment of the mortgage there would still be a balance payable to Tom. Until the sum insured and profits reached £60,000 a decreasing term insurance would operate to ensure a sufficient sum insured in the event of his premature death. The endowment premium plus the term insurance premium would be cheaper than the quotation above.

In reply to Mr Smith's enquiry about using the lump sum from his pension plan to pay off the mortgage they confirmed that he could arrange to do that. They agreed that it would be cheaper for him as he would be allowed income tax relief on the premium. However, they said, the Inland Revenue quite rightly feel that a pension is for that purpose and should not be used for any other.

He also enquired about a "low start" plan. They explained that this simply meant reducing some of the earlier payments and adding the balance to the outstanding sum. Monthly payments would increase annually to reach maximum after five years.

If Mr Smith decided to obtain a mortgage using a building society repayment plan he could also effect a term insurance so that in the event of his death before the mortgage was repaid he would not leave his dependants a mortgage to repay.

Pensions

Self-employed persons and those in non-pensionable employment have, since 1956, been allowed tax relief if they wished to buy a retirement annuity in instalments. The object was to bring them into line with those on occupational pension schemes. Existing contracts are not affected but no new ones may now be incepted. Annuities purchased must commence at ages between 60 and 75. Policies cannot be surrendered.

Personal pensions may now be bought by all who are not members of an occupational pension scheme, whether self-employed or not. As far as employers are concerned, although they may continue to offer an occupational pension scheme to employees, this cannot be made a condition of employment.

No employer is compelled to offer an occupational pension scheme nor to contribute to an employee's personal pension plan. Within the limits shown below those effecting a personal pension will be entitled to full tax relief on the premiums paid:

Age at beginning tax year	Maximum contribution as a percentage of earnings	
35 or under	17½%	
36–45	20%	Up to
46–50	25%	5% may
51–55	30%	be invested
56–60	35%	in life
61+	40%	insurance

Based on maximum earnings of £60,000

Employees who decide on a personal pension will not only receive part of the National Insurance contribution paid by employer and employee towards their pension but a Government incentive until 5.4.93. Employees may still continue in the Government scheme (SERPS — State Earnings Related Pension Scheme) and add a personal pension to it.

Anyone changing jobs can invest the transfer value available from his or her late employers in a personal pension scheme. Both employers and employees who have not invested the maximum contribution over the last six years can do so in the current tax year.

Pensions from the policyholder's own contribution can be taken between ages 50 and 75. Part cash of up to 25% can be taken with a maximum of £90,000. Pensions arising from the rebated National Insurance contributions are called "protected rights". No part of these can be taken in cash but they can be used in the calculations of the fund from which the 25% is allowed in cash. That part of the pension based on protected rights cannot be taken before the state retirement age.

For a small additional premium it is possible to insure so that the premiums are still credited even though the insured is unable to work as a result of accident or disease from six months up to retirement age.

Employers may arrange for additional contributions from members of their occupational pension scheme limited to the percentages listed above. These are called Additional Voluntary Contributions (AVCs). Alternatively members of a scheme can contribute to separate schemes of their choice called "free-standing" AVCs.

Approved pension providers include insurers, unit trusts and building societies. At the present time the insurers, with their many years of experience in this field, still hold the advantage. Pensions based on life insurance with a profit element must still be the favourite. Even the stock market crash of 1987 has not had much effect on the profits being distributed.

The new rules allow for the transfer of funds from one pension provider to another at the vesting date. This means that those about to retire can consider where the money they have saved will earn the most income for them.

Loan back facilities

Loans may be available through many personal schemes. First introduced for the self-employed, these loans are intended for repayment
from the proceeds of the tax free commutation at retirement. The
interest may be added to the debt for repayment or paid annually.
The loan may be for any purpose.

Pension mortgages

A logical development from the loan back facility is the pension mortgage. A mortgage is obtained in which interest is only paid during its
term. A pension scheme is effected which will provide a pension at a
a given age, plus a tax free lump sum. The lump sum must exceed
the mortgage debt and the contract will be used as collateral for the
mortgage. When the pension becomes due the lump sum will repay
the mortgage.

As mentioned earlier, this type of mortgage restricts the cash sum
available at retirement and, for that reason, should be used with
caution.

It is also becoming possible to mix a pension mortgage and an
endowment mortgage if the maturity dates coincide. If the endowment
matures earlier than the pension the proceeds must be left on deposit
with the life office until the pension becomes available. Interest willl,
of course, be paid.

It is also possible to repay a mortgage using the AVCs mentioned
earlier in this section

Permanent health insurance

One of the disadvantages of personal accident insurance is that it is
renewable annually. This gives insurers the opportunity to refuse to
accept renewal or to seek to impose new terms. In addition, the period
during which weekly benefits are paid is restricted, usually to 104
weeks. Insurers have the power to cancel a personal accident insurance
at any time, although very seldom exercise the option.

These disadvantages are overcome in permanent health insurance.
Policies are automatically renewed (as in life insurance) so long as the

renewal premium is paid. Furthermore, benefits may continue until the expiry date of the insurance — usually age 60 or 65.

The premium is based on age at entry, as in life insurance. Age must be proved and a medical examination could be sought, although sometimes the cover is arranged in conjunction with a life insurance.

Most policies are for "disability", which is defined in the policy as "inability to follow one's usual occupation". It can be seen that this is not as restrictive as "inability to follow any occupation". Before accepting an insurance insurers try to assess the probable loss of income. In order to encourage an early return to work they will only offer insurance for a percentage of the probable income, assuming the addition of State benefits. Percentages allowed vary between 50% and 75%.

Discounts are allowed for voluntary excesses. Thus benefits could be deferred for periods from one month to one or two years. For an additional premium some insurers are prepared to include increased benefits after an agreed period and index linked benefit.

Example

Mr Brown ran the local newsagent and confectioners with the help of Mrs Brown. He was worried that if he fell sick his wife would not be able to cope and the shop would have to be shut. He reasoned that many of his regular customers would transfer their custom to Wilson's. Furthermore, he would have problems with the newsagency.

After a discussion with his insurance broker he effected a permanent health insurance with weekly benefits of £250 — sufficient to pay for a temporary manager. As Mrs Brown felt she would be able to cope on her own for six weeks he had benefits deferred for that period.

An insurer who previously offered insurance against "drink driving" disqualification (see the *Introduction*) no longer offers that cover and moved into health insurance. Cover is available against loss of driving licences as a result of ill-health. Death whilst driving is also covered by the new policies.

Group permanent health insurance

This type of insurance could be used to enable employers to pay their staff during periods of prolonged absence due to sickness or accident. Employees will also be enabled to continue membership of the employer's pension scheme (and, if applicable, group life insurance). If a substantial deferment is obtained the premium can be kept fairly low.

In the event of permanent disability an employee can be paid a salary until retirement date when he or she will receive a full pension.

Some insurers will accept groups without individual proposal forms if there are more than 25 employees and eventually all are covered. Many insurers stipulate 50 employees as a minimum. There are non-medical limits, as insurers are concerned about individuals earning far more than the average salary. Usually employees over 55 or with less than 5 years before retirement are not accepted.

Both premiums and benefits paid to employees are acceptable business expenses. Employees are taxed on income received.

Employees may be covered under a voluntary scheme to which they pay premiums to the employer who transmits them to the insurer in bulk. Each policy is underwritten separately by the insurer who allows a discount for the number of employees included in the insurance. There are non-medical limits and an upper age limit at entry of age 50. There is no tax relief in respect of premiums paid and benefits are tax free until they have been paid for a full financial year.

In all types of permanent health insurance payment of premiums during incapacity may be included in the policy cover for a very small extra premium.

Medical expenses insurance

This is a rapidly growing market in the United Kingdom, providing as it does for payment of hospital and nursing home charges, surgical operations, anaesthetists, physiotherapy, consultations with specialists and home nursing. Some insurers also offer medical insurance in conjunction with permanent health insurance.

For the business person it is almost essential to have the ability to be able to obtain a specialist's opinion without waiting for a hospital appointment which could be offered for an inconvenient time. Both the self-employed and senior employees, who are to be admitted to hospital, need to be able to select when to go. The use of a private room and a telephone enables them to retain contact with the business.

From April 1990 those paying premiums in respect of medical insurance on persons over 60 years of age will be able to benefit from a tax rebate on those premiums, deducted at source.

An employer who is paying an employee's salary during incapacity will benefit from the existence of private medical insurance. It will ensure that the period of absence is kept to a minimum.

For those employing less than 50 employees discounts are allowed and, with employees paying towards their own policies, the costs can be reduced.

Questions and answers

Q On my insurance policy it states that I am covered for "riot". What is a riot? Must there be a mob on the loose for there to be a riot?

A No. The number of people involved was recently increased by law from 3 to 12. If a group of that size or larger gathered together to take some sort of action and began to do so — sufficiently to disturb someone of reasonable courage (in the example given above it was a policeman) that would be a riot. It could be for any of a number of reasons. Those involved do not have to intend occupying the local Town Hall or Whitehall.

Q I am a boilermaker and have £100,000 worth of goods which I want to insure against fire and theft. When I complained about the premium the agent said that I could insure for theft on a "first loss" basis. Could you explain?

A If the contents of your premises consist mainly of large, heavy goods, and you feel that most of them are unlikely to be stolen at any one time you can insure for the sum you think is likely to be taken on one occasion. The insurers will usually increase the rate per cent. Provided you do not have considerably more goods than you have declared they will pay any losses up to the sum insured.

Q I have read the term "subject to average" on my insurance policies. What exactly does it mean?

A There is more than one type of "average" clause in insurance. There are special ones for agricultural risks, for example. The phrase itself means that if, at the time of a loss the insured property at risk is more than the sum insured, insurers will only pay a proportion of the loss. They calculate the relationship between the sum insured and the value at risk and apply it to the loss. The reason for applying average is because they have not received the full premium for the amount insured and, therefore, treat you as your own insurer for the difference.

Example — sum insured = £100,000   Loss £80,000
Total value of stock at time of loss = £200,000
Adjustment = $\dfrac{\text{Sum insured}}{\text{Value of stock}} \times \text{loss} = \dfrac{£100,000 \times £80,000}{£200,000}$

$$= £40,000$$

Q In the text you state that among the exclusions under a "goods in transit" insurance are "watches and clocks". I repair watches and clocks for the trade and I wish to insure them against fire and theft when collecting and delivering them.
A There are many exclusions in insurance policies because they are designed to offer basic cover required by the majority at an acceptable premium. In many cases the restrictions can be removed for an extra premium. There are insurers who specialise in your particular trade and will be advertising in your trade journal.

Q It is compulsory to have employers' liability insurance but, as we are a family business, does it apply to us?
A The legal requirements of employers' liability insurance do not apply if the employer is the father, mother, husband, wife, grandparent, child or step-child, brother or sister or half-brother or half-sister of the employee.

Q Am I liable if one of my employees injures another employee?
A Yes. I am afraid you are. You are liable for the personal negligence of an employee or the negligence of an employee in carrying out your business. Even if employees agree to do something which goes wrong you are liable. The law requires you to take reasonable care in selecting employees to see that they are competent. As soon as you find them incompetent you must take suitable action. Training is one way of dealing with incompetence. Improved super-

vision may be another. Special care is essential in appointing fore-men and managers. Bad habits (eg practical jokes) must be dealt with by disciplinary action immediately.

Your employers' liability insurers will deal with claims made against you in respect of personal injury. Claims from other traders or the public will be dealt with by your public liability insurers. There is an obvious advantage in arranging both types of insurance with the same insurer.

Q I cannot afford public liability insurance for my small grocery shop. Anyway I am very careful and the only incident in the shop wasn't my fault — a customer spilled some yoghurt over the floor and another customer slipped on it.

A The cost of public liability insurance is very small but essential. Your potential liability can run into many thousands or even hundreds of thousands of pounds; even successfully defending a claim against you could be costly. You may not recover all, or even any, of your costs. If you have a public liability insurance your insurers will take over, deal with and pay compensation and any costs involved.

If anyone is injured in your shop, and some injuries could be serious, you could be liable. Goods badly displayed or moved about by customers could fall on other customers' heads. Polythene bags dropped on the floor or spilled foods (like yoghurt) on which customers slip could be your liability unless you can prove that you have a regular system of checks. That could be very difficult. If a claim is allowed to reach the courts you may obtain bad local publicity. Even the major supermarkets find it necessary to settle doubtful claims on "nuisance" value.

Q My broker has suggested the addition of "family liability" insurance to my policy. The premium is very small but what sort of liability is there for my children or animals?

A Children do have legal liability for their own negligence. There have been claims in respect of broken bus windows caused by negligence. One case concerned the capping of teeth damaged by a snooker ball hit from a table in a youth club. A dog, known to chase cyclists, was allowed to escape and caused a cyclist to swerve into the path of a car that went through a hedge in taking avoiding action and caused a fatal accident.

Q What do I include in the total "contents" for my shopkeeper's insurance?

A The total should include stock, any improvements you have carried out to the premises (if you are a tenant), the cost of re-writing your business books, all clothing and personal effects of you and your employees (this sum is usually a very limited one), business fixtures and fittings and your equipment. It is also suggested that you allow for inflation in the coming year in your calculations.

Q I have heard from others in the fashion business that insurers did not pay full value when assessing a loss. How is a loss of fashion goods assessed?

A The usual way of calculating a loss of goods under an insurance policy is by reference to the list price. The selling price includes your profit and would not be a correct basis to use. A true indemnity is based on the cost of the goods to you. However, in the fashion trade goods depreciate in value due to rapid changes in fashion. Insurers, therefore, will wish to calculate the value of such goods at the depreciated price, if it is less than the original list price.

Q I have some small but fairly expensive goods in my shop window. Should I obtain special insurance against "smash and grab"?

A Your theft insurance covers all forms of "violent and forcible" entry to your premises. Unless specifically excluded this would include "smash and grab" raiders. It is not essential for the thief to actually put his or her whole body into the building for entry to be violent and forcible.

Q My fidelity guarantee policy stipulates that I must report a loss to the police. I have made a claim under the policy but the employee has promised to repay the sum he has stolen over two years, if I do not prosecute him. Why do insurers still insist that he be prosecuted?

A In theft cases insurers always insist on the matter being reported to the police. If the wording of your policy does not actually state this it will imply it by words, such as "take every possible step to recover the loss". The obvious way of doing that is by notifying the police.

In dealing with a fidelity guarantee loss it could be compounding the crime for the insured to reach an agreement with the thief that if he or she agreed to repay over two years no action would be taken against him or her. Insurers would not wish to see him or her imprisoned, however, but put on probation and employed by someone who will make sure that the instalments are paid back as promised (and, probably, imposed by the court).

Q I have a private car insurance that allows anyone authorised by me to drive. Recently, whilst the van was being serviced, my employee used the car to call on a customer. He had a slight accident and the insurers refused to indemnify me. I am not clear about the reason.

A I would presume that you have a basic policy (insurers generally call it Class A or Class 1). This allows use on your business but only whilst you are present in the car (whether you are driving or not). You will need a Class B (or Class 2) insurance which allows business use. This will usually cost you about 25% more per year.

Q My brother's private car insurance was restricted to driving by him and his wife. Recently, whilst mine was off the road, he said I could borrow his car. I rang my insurance broker who told me that my motor insurance allowed me to drive a vehicle not belonging to me. However, after an accident a police officer looked at my insurance certificate and was satisfied but my insurers will not pay for the damage to the car. Why not?

A Your motor insurance policy has an extension which allows you to drive a vehicle not belonging to you. However, the cover whilst you are driving that other vehicle is for third party only. The police officer was satisfied with this because that is the cover required by law.

Your insurance broker should have arranged the temporary addition of the borrowed car to your motor insurance policy. The alternative would be for your brother to have arranged to add you to the drivers named on his insurance just for a few days. There would have been a small charge for the service in either case.

Q Recently I bought a second car which was added to my motor insurance policy. At renewal this year I found that although I am allowed a no claim discount of 60% the added vehicle was only allowed one year's no claim discount. Both vehicles are in my name with driving restricted to me. I do not understand the agent's explanation.

A Briefly, although insurers seek information about your driving experience before insuring you, the discounts you earn are attached to the particular car insured. Each car added to your policy is accepted at full premium (ie without a discount) and must earn a discount over the years. It is possible, eventually, that both your cars will have a full discount allowed.

If you sell the first car insurers will usually allow the discount to be transferred to the second car.

In the circumstances you mention (ie driving restricted to you only) insurers should allow a discount from the third party section of the insurance as you obviously cannot drive both cars at once.

Q I had a travel insurance when abroad last year. My camera was stolen whilst I was sitting at a beachside cafe. The insurers did not pay for the loss as they said I should have reported it to the police. My friends also told me that I should have claimed for my trousers which were ripped when I slipped down a cliff. But I disagree as they are not baggage. Please comment on these two matters.

A If you suffer any losses, at home or abroad, you must take all possible steps to recover the loss. This, in practice, even if the wording does not specifically say so, means reporting the matter to the police. If the loss happens abroad try to get written proof (even if you cannot read it) to bring back for insurers.

Your friends are correct about the damage to your trousers. The policy is virtually an all risks cover on your clothes, whether worn or in suitcases, and personal effects.

Q I am told that I can only insure my own life and that of my wife or someone who owes me money. One of my neighbours says that he has insured his parents. Is that possible?

A Yes. Family relationship does not give you the right to insure. However, the State allows a small insurance (up to £30 on each life) on the lives of parents, step-parents and grandparents. This interest is created under the Industrial Assurance and Friendly Societies Acts 1948/58. These insurances are effected through industrial assurance agents (home service representatives).

Q You say that if a policyholder is willing to pay a slightly higher life insurance premium he or she can have a share in the profits of the insurer. Is it worthwhile doing this?

A Even when the stock markets are not doing too well the long term investments of life insurers are pretty sound. This means that the annual bonus is unlikely to be affected. The additional bonus (usually called a "terminal bonus", which is added at the end of the term or at death) could be reduced if the stock market does not improve. Over many years the bonuses have always exceeded the additional premium. Insurers must be careful not to quote future bonuses but they can tell you what has been paid up to date. Many insurers can show that they have paid twice the sum insured, without taking the terminal bonus into consideration, for a twenty year insurance. This is far in excess of the additional premium charged.

If the insurance is unit linked then the value of the insurance can be checked regularly and is entirely dependent on the situation in the investment market. It is possible to do much better but equally possible to find that the profit is lower than anticipated.

CHAPTER 3

Insurance Packages

Traders' combined insurances

In the previous chapters details were given of the many classes of insurance available in the British insurance market. All of these are obtainable directly from insurers or through intermediaries. Most leading insurers offer packages for traders. Some of these are general packages but the requirements of specific trades can be included in additional cover. Other insurers offer separate packages designed for shopkeepers, offices, hotels and boarding houses, engineering works, small builders and so on.

These carry titles such as shop insurance, retailer insurance, shopkeeper's all-in policy, commercial plus insurance, tradesmen's combined insurance, trader's single rate insurance, retailer's combined insurance and many, many more. In this chapter the packages available to the trader will be examined in some detail. Two facts must, however, be noted. The first is that this information is only intended to be a guide to be used in selecting suitable cover. The intermediary exists to place insurances in the most suitable market. Competition results in changes in cover and practices within insurance. A good intermediary will be aware of them.

It is not possible to define the term "good intermediary". Most can recommend insurers, assist in completion of the proposal form and point to possible "gaps" in cover which require additional protection. The testing time will arrive when a loss occurs. Has the proper advice been given and is the insured fully covered in respect of the loss? Has the insurance been placed with an insurer who is prompt, efficient and fair in handling claims? Recommendation is the safest way of obtaining a suitable intermediary when considering placing insurances. The only persons who can offer a recommendation based on experience are those who have been claimants. They have tasted the pudding and can offer advice based on that experience.

Traders benefit from a package because many of the gaps in cover between policies are closed. There is one renewal date, one set of insurance documents and one premium to pay. Most insurers offer facilities for instalment premiums and offer the business a tailored insurance. Thus there is "standard" cover to which may be added a range of additional items.

Package cover

Trade contents

Most policies describe what they mean by trade contents. A usual definition would be " . . . belonging to the insured or for which he is liable". This would include:

  (a) stock in trade and goods in trust;
  (b) trade fixtures and fittings, machinery and other contents, including the shop front (excluding glass), blinds, signs, pedal cycles, clothing and personal effects of the insured and his or her employees, up to £x maximum per person;
  (c) landlord's fixtures and fittings and interior decorations for which the insured is responsible.

The sum insured for personal effects can vary from £100 to £250, with or without a single item limit. Some policies refer to "directors' and partners' personal effects" only. Policies may include other items such as furniture, books and stationery. If business books or records are included, the cover, in this section, does not include rewriting costs.

Generally separate sums insured are required in respect of the separation of the contents as listed above. Most shopkeeper's insurances allow for 20% extra stock to be on the premises at certain times of the year. This applies to November and December. In some cases the extension includes the January sales and extends to mid-January. Other insurers offer 20% or 25% extra cover for three months free but will allow increased sums insured up to 200% for an additional premium. For traders selling liquor the additional cover could be as high as 50% of the stock figure, without charge, for November, December and early January and, in addition, for 14 days prior to a public holiday.

Most insurances offer index linking and some povide for replacement on a "new for old" basis — except for stock.

Fire and special perils

This is sometimes listed as "contents cover". In addition to insurance against fire or lightning there is cover against:

explosion;
aircraft, aerial devices or articles dropped therefrom;
earthquake;
riot, civil commotion and malicious persons;
storm, tempest, flood, bursting of waterpipes;
subterranean fire;
impact by road vehicles or animals;
sprinkler leakage;
escape of oil used for central heating;
breakage or collapse of radio or television aerials other than satellite dishes;
falling trees.

In respect of malicious damage, storm, tempest, flood and burst pipes and damage caused by vehicles or animals in the insured's ownership or control, the first £100–250 of any claim is usually excluded. Some insurers offer "accidental damage" cover for an additional premium. This would exclude stock and could also be subject to the excess.

Theft and robbery

This covers theft or attempted theft following upon forcible and violent entry or followed by such exit. Usually subject to an excess of £100.

Also covered is hold-up by violence and/or threats of violence to the insured and/or employees.

There are requirements involving the setting of security devices (if stipulated) and that the drawers of cash registers are left open when they are not in use or the shop is closed for business.

Business interruption, consequential loss or loss of profits

Cover is offered against loss of the profits of the business following an insured claim. In addition, many policies extend to cover losses caused by the difficulty of public access to the premises (caused by a fire or other insured event in the vicinity, such as a gas leak, bomb hoax or snow), infectious or contagious diseases, murder, suicide, food poisoning, closure by local authorities due to defective sanitation or breakdown of public utilities (for example power failure lasting more than 30 minutes), and loss or damage at supplier's premises.

Most policies cover lost profits over a period of twelve months but longer periods are available for an additional premium.

Cover is obtainable in respect of loss of income following the loss of a liquor licence, including the costs and expenses of an appeal.

Legal liability

In some instances separate sections are provided for public liability, employers' liability and product liability, with extensions for certain additional cover. The indemnity for employers' liability is unlimited in amount but restricted to £1M in respect of public and product liability, although some insurers have a much lower standard limit

Included in the term "employee" are self-employed labour only sub-contractors, employees on loan from another employer and those on work experience schemes.

Cover also includes claims in respect of treatment given in a professional capacity and in respect of claims for wrongful arrest of alleged shoplifters. The indemnities in these cases are limited to £250,000 and £10,000 (sometimes £25,000) respectively.

The costs of legal expenses incurred are also included in the cover in each case. Some insurers require an additional premium for cover in respect of professional claims.

Glass

This provides for the replacement of broken glass and, if necessary, temporary boarding up. Included in the cover are window frames as well as fittings or displays also damaged by the breakage of the glass. The monetary value of the glass is not normally stated but there are monetary limits of £500 in respect of the damage caused. Some insurers may include lettering on glass up to £200.

Cover may include mirrors, lavatory pans and wash basins for which the insured is responsible as a tenant.

Money

Money, a term which is defined in most policies (see below), is insured against loss. Some policies use the terms " . . . by any cause, except . . . " and follow with exceptions, which are normally dishonesty of employees or from unattended vehicles. In respect of loss caused by dishonesty of an employee insurers may accept the claim if notified within a stated period of 7 to 15 days.

Other insurers list the possible situations in which loss of money is covered and the maximum sum in respect of any one loss. They will include:

(a) the saleshop or other premises during business hours or in a locked safe, outside business hours (limit of £1000–£2500);

(b) at the homes of partners, directors or employees (limit of £500–£1000);

(c) in transit or in a bank night safe (limit £1000–£2500).

The definition of money is generally cash, bank and currency notes, cheques, giro cheques, postal and money orders, crossed bankers' drafts, crossed giro drafts, current postage stamps, unused units in postage stamp franking machines, National Insurance stamps, National Savings and holiday-with-pay stamps, National Savings certificates, premium bonds, luncheon vouchers, debit and credit cash sales vouchers, trading stamps, gift tokens, consumer redemption vouchers and VAT purchase invoices.

Much higher limits of £100,000 to £250,000 are given in respect of the loss of crossed bank and giro cheques, crossed money orders, crossed bankers' and giro bank drafts, unexpired units in franking machines, stamped National Insurance cards, National Savings certificates and premium bonds, debit and credit card sales vouchers and VAT purchase invoices.

Cover may include damage caused by theft or attempted theft to a safe, strong room, case, bag or waistcoat used for carrying money.

Compensation is paid for death or disablement caused by assault as well as for the loss or damage to personal effects belonging to directors, partners or employees following assault.

Compensation for death or the loss of limbs or eyes caused by assault or as a direct result of theft or attempted theft may be £5000–£10,000. Weekly benefits during disablement — £50–£100 per week for 104 weeks maximum. In some cases policies restrict benefits to employees between 16 and 70 years of age. Damage to personal effects is limited to £250–£500.

Certain restrictions are imposed. One is that the keys to a safe or the details of combinations must not be left on the premises when they are closed for business. In the case of larger organisations the stipulation may refer to " . . . that part of the premises . . . "

Additional cover

The requirements of different trades and businesses vary and, in order to accommodate them, insurers offer additional cover or, if necessary, separate policies to add to the package. It is usual for there to be increases in the sum quoted above and insurers may:
  (a) refuse to extend cover;
  (b) require additional protections or make stipulations before quoting to extend cover;
  (c) quote to extend cover.
Below are listed some of the forms of insurance available to be added to traders' packages. Excesses of £50 (in some circumstances £100) apply. The list is not exhaustive and, if specific requirements are not listed, the intermediary or insurer should be approached.

Buildings

The building, if owned, may be insured against:
  (a) fire, lightning, explosion, earthquake;
  (b) impact by vehicle or animals;
  (c) riot, civil commotion, strikers locked out, workers or persons taking part in labour disturbances and malicious persons;
  (d) leakage of fuel oil or beer;
  (e) burglary or attempted burglary, involving breaking into or out of the buildings by violent and forcible means;
  (f) storm and flood;
  (g) escape of water from fixed water apparatus;
  (h) falling television and radio aerials, fittings and masts;
  (i) falling trees;

(j) accidental damage to underground service pipes;

(k) loss of rent — usually restricted to 10% of sum insured;

(l) property owner's liability under s. 3 of the Defective Premises Act 1972, up to £1M.

The sum insured should include:

(a) the costs of removing debris, dismantling, demolishing and shoring up the property;

(b) additional costs of reinstatement of the buildings to comply with building regulations and bye-laws;

(c) architects' and surveyors' fees.

All risks cover may be given. In that case the hazards will not be listed, although excesses applying to particular ones will be stated individually.

Frozen food or food spoilage

If a refrigerator or deep freeze unit breaks down or is damaged the contents may deteriorate. Cover is given for loss resulting from breakdown, explosion, non-operation of thermostat, refrigerant fumes or failure of the electricity supply (unless caused by strike action).

There may be an excess of £25 or £50 and wilful action of an employee is excluded.

Goods in transit

There is a variation in the forms of cover available. Cover may be for collection and delivery of goods but excluding burglary, robbery, storm and flood risks, theft by employees and losses from unattended vehicles.

One insurer is prepared to include losses from an unattended vehicle during working hours if all doors and windows are securely locked. Outside working hours the cover is only available if the vehicle is in a locked garage. Specific mention is made of loss or damage to tarpaulins, skips and trolleys whilst in transit. Drivers' personal effects may also be covered for small sums.

Some policies specifically include the loading and unloading risk and state that the vehicle must be owned or operated by the insured. In most cases rates per cent are quoted but there are policies with fixed sums insured that may be increased for an extra premium. As an example, one insurer quotes limits of £1500–£2500 per vehicle and £1000 maximum per single loss.

Policies are available which extend cover in respect of goods sent by road carrier, rail or post. Cover includes goods on a dockside or in a dockside warehouse for up to 30 days, if sent under fob conditions (which means that the consignment is not otherwise insured under a marine insurance policy).

Rates are usually based on:

(a) a rate per vehicle in respect of goods transported in the insured's own vehicles, with a maximum loss per vehicle;

(b) a rate per cent based on the estimated total value of goods in transit per annum. There would be a maximum per consignment.

Fidelity guarantee or dishonesty of employees

Not all insurers include this form of cover in a package but are willing to offer insurance separately, with renewal at the same time as the package, if required.

The cover is simply against loss of money (sometimes including other property) resulting from dishonesty or fraud of employees. Limits of £10,000, usually subject to excesses of £100–£250, are mentioned but higher limits may be obtained.

Losses must be discovered within 24 months of cover ceasing in respect of the employee or the policy expiry. A system of check may be agreed and cover may be in respect of each employee or all employees.

Personal accident and sickness insurance

Cover is provided in respect of named persons for accidental bodily injury and may be based on a unit providing £1000–£2000 in the event of death, loss of eyes or sight or limbs or total disablement. Included in the cover is a weekly benefit of £10 and a medical expenses payment of 15% of the total weekly benefit claimed. A similar weekly benefit is also available in respect of inability to work due to sickness.

Multiples of a unit may be obtained for each individual so long as the weekly benefit does not exceed the weekly income. In respect of employees, and bearing in mind social security benefits available, weekly benefits should be limited to about 50% or 60% of weekly average earnings.

As there are various personal accident and permanent health policies available some insurers offer a basic policy providing a sum of £5000 in respect of death or permanent disablement of the insured or an employee.

Different definitions are used in respect of disablement. The weekly benefit is paid if the claimant is "unable to follow his usual occupation". The total disablement benefit will only be paid if the claimant "is unable to follow any occupation".

There are many exclusions relating to sporting activities, motor cycling and the use of machinery. Some of the exclusions can be removed in respect of individuals for an additional premium.

Loss of book debts

The cover offered here is intended to operate if the insured's books, records or invoices are lost, destroyed, stolen or damaged and as a result he or she is unable to trace outstanding debts. The documents may have been on the insured's premises, other premises not occupied by the insured or in transit. If the loss involves computer systems there are exclusions but not in respect of any erasure or distortion caused by lightning.

An alternative policy offers cover in respect of either loss or damage caused by fire or listed special perils or the full cover specified above.

The cover is in respect of the value of the untraced money plus any agreed costs involved in tracing debtors. Accountants' fees in proving the loss will also be paid, providing they do not exceed the loss.

Some insurers stipulate that outstanding debt totals must be kept at other premises.

All risks

The headings under which this cover may be found will vary. The section is intended to provide an indemnity in respect of loss or damage to office equipment, including telephones, whilst on the premises. Extension of cover to other premises may be obtained. The exclusions relate to mechanical and electrical breakdown and there is usually an excess of £25.

An alternative insurance offers "all risks" cover based on a schedule of insured items. The exclusions are similar to the policy described above.

General remarks

Some insurers list the maximum sums insured and the trades acceptable for the packages offered. Others mention trades for which cover is not available. In particular, most packages are not offered to jewellers, pawnbrokers, furriers, video dealers or betting shops. In many cases alternative schemes are possible.

Most policies have minimum sums insured of £10,000, with upper limits which may be in respect of £250,000 for stock and £350,000 in respect of buildings. Special terms may be offered for insuring ten or more shops or for agreeing to renew the insurance for three years.

Premiums may be based on minimum cover for each section and additional premiums for increased cover and extra sections. Alternatively each type of insurance may be rated separately.

Policies are usually index linked. The General Building Cost Index of the Royal Institute of Chartered Surveyors is applied in respect of buildings and the Producer Price Index for Home Sales of Manufactured Products issued by the Department of Trade and Industry for stock and other contents.

Excesses vary from insurer to insurer. Although excesses have been mentioned in this text, insurers' practice is changing all the time to meet competition or to deal with a higher than expected incidence of claims. In most cases a business can negotiate discounts if it is willing to increase the amount of excess it is prepared to accept.

A good basis on which to consider excesses is that of the smallest loss that would be the subject of a claim. If, for example, a trader feels that any claim below £200 may be difficult to prove or not worth the time involved then an excess of £200 could be negotiated.

A separate policy is available for motor traders. Motor trade policies are divided into those covering road risks and others in respect of premises risks. The Motor Traders' Comprehensive Road and Garage Insurance includes both internal and road risks cover with many additional items of cover for traders. These include theft of vehicles from the premises, comprehensive cover on vehicles garaged away from the premises, tuition and demonstration cover, fuel installations, malicious damage and pleasure use of vehicles by the spouse of a partner or director.

Businesses in inner cities experiencing difficulty in obtaining insurance cover should refer to the section headed "Business Insurance in Inner Cities".

Household insurances

Fire insurance became available to householders in London shortly after the Great Fire of 1666 and was more generally available during the eighteenth century. By the end of the nineteenth century insurance could be obtained against burglary. Most people required fire insurance cover but many householders also took advantage of the existence of burglary insurance to effect cover against both fire and burglary. Some insurers, to encourage this development, offered a combined fire and burglary insurance. After the second world war the "householder's comprehensive" insurance arrived on the market. The term "comprehensive" was an unfortunate one as the policy was simply a fire and theft insurance with a number of additional perils. Competition and the advent of modern technology increased the policy content, and this development is still continuing.

Today most general insurers offer a "household insurance" — the term "comprehensive" has slowly slipped away. An important distinction exists between that insurance and an "all risks" policy. The latter does truly attempt to cover, in one policy, all insurable risks. The household insurance lists the hazards against which cover is given and is, of necessity, limited in scope.

Some insurers sell household insurance under a brand name; there are many on the market, such as, *House Plus, Hearth and Home, Homesure, Home Insurance.*

There are policies covering the contents of a flat or house only suitable for tenants, and others include building cover and are designed for owner-occupiers. Although there are some variations, most of the policies available are divided into separate sections. In addition to the basic cover, options are available, such as "all risks" or cover for freezers or even caravans.

Competition has encouraged insurers to innovate but the cover generally available is outlined below.

Buildings insurance

Included in the definition of "buildings" is the house with its fixtures and fittings, the garage and domestic outbuildings, swimming pool, walls, gates, fences, paths, drives and terraces. Cover is given against damage caused by fire, lightning, explosion, earthquake, riot and malicious damage, aircraft and other aerial devices and objects falling therefrom, and impact by animals and road or rail vehicles.

Included in the cover is damage caused by theft or attempted theft, falling trees or aerials (some policies include street lighting standards and telegraph poles), escape of water from tanks or pipes, escape of oil from central heating, flood and storm, subsidence, landslip or heave and accidental damage to underground pipes or cables (supplying electricity, gas, oil or water, and sewage pipes).

Accidental breakage of glass used in windows, doors and skylights is included, as is damage to baths, basins and washbasins. Some insurers include built-in furniture and fixed floor, ceiling and wall coverings (excluding carpets).

Most insurers impose an excess in respect of "water damage" (that is loss or damage caused by water escaping from pipes and tanks or resulting from storm or flood. This figure has usually been £15. There are insurers who now impose excesses in all sections to prevent small claims or allow discount for excesses of, say, £50 or £100. Cover usually includes emergency work such as protection with tarpaulins. Substantial excesses are imposed in respect of claims for subsidence, heave and landslip. The sum may be £500 or a proportion of the actual claim.

The owner is insured in respect of his or her legal liability as owner (and not as occupier in this section). The limit may well be £½M to £1M plus legal costs. Liability arising out of a business or profession is excluded. The insured is covered in respect of his or her legal liability under the Defective Premises Act 1972 to previous private premises owned or the present building for up to seven years after cancellation of the policy.

If the premises become uninhabitable as a result of an insured peril, the insurers will pay the cost of temporary accommodation and reimburse any loss of rent. There is a limit in this section which could be as much as 20% of the sum insured.

If, at the time of a loss, a contract has been signed to sell the property the purchaser will be entitled to the benefit of the insurance. The provisos are that he or she completes the sale and that the property has not been insured by him or her.

Fees charged by architects or surveyors in connection with reinstatement of the building are included. The insurance also covers the costs of shoring up and removal of debris following a loss. Any additional costs resulting from the need to comply with statutory or local authority regulations will be met.

The sum insured should be based on the rebuilding costs and not the market price — which includes the land value. The Association of British Insurers advise the use of the chart provided by the Royal Institution of Chartered Surveyors (copies free from the ABI).

Contents insurance

The contents include household goods, appliances, furniture, clothing, food and drink, televisions, computers, audio equipment, videos, jewellery, pictures, ornaments, money and personal effects, the property of the insured and members of his or her family. Also included is property not belonging to the family but for which they are legally responsible (things like hired televisions or telephones). Most things fixed to the property permanently are considered to be part of the building, although carpets are regarded as contents.

The "home" includes property in the house, garage and outbuildings (for example, tools kept in sheds). Usually there are exclusions in respect of cars, boats, cheques, credit cards, pets and livestock.

The perils against which the contents are insured are as listed above under "buildings insurance". There are not usually specific excesses applied to "water" damage although, to keep premiums under control, a general excess may be applied to the policy as a whole.

The theft cover is restricted, if the property is let, to "breaking into or out of" the premises. This is not quite as restrictive as "violent and forcible" entry or exit. The cover is also restricted in respect of theft of insured property from any other building, to breaking in or out of the premises.

The accidental breakage of glass cover is for mirrors, fixed glass in furniture and glass tops to the latter. It may include ceramic hobs. Often included in accidental damage cover are televisions, computers and audio or video equipment.

If the insured is a tenant and not owner of the property then the policy is extended to cover damage to fixtures and fittings belonging to the landlord or installed permanently by the insured. Included in this are decorations and accidental damage to fixed glass, toilets, wash basins and baths, and underground services (as listed in the buildings insurance). Where excesses are applied in the buildings insurance they will be applied in this section of the tenant's insurance.

The legal liability of a tenant as occupier or an owner as occupier is covered with an upper limit of £½M or £1M. Most policies extend the cover to the insured and his or her family in their everyday affairs away from the home. The exclusions would involve business or professional matters or the driving of motor vehicles.

The cost of alternative accommodation is also included in the insurance with an upper limit, usually, of 20% of the sum insured.

There are, of course, overlaps in cover where the insured is both owner and occupier of the house.

The sum insured should be the total replacement value of all the property in the home, including sheds and garages. The way in which insurers settle claims under household properties depends on the type of insurance effected. The terms of the insurance may stipulate that the sum insured represents the full value of the property insured. This means, in effect, that serious under-insurance at the time of a loss would invalidate the policy. In practice insurers would seek the insured's agreement to apply average. It is becoming more common for insurers to insert an average clause similar to business insurances.

Subject to the sum insured being sufficient, an insurance based on indemnity will pay the cost of replacing the items lost or damaged with a deduction for "wear and tear". This is a difficult concept and a source of much bargaining and dissatisfaction. The basis is a rule of thumb application — say, 20% a year for wear on clothes, perhaps more for bed linen and less for carpets and furniture. To reduce the items to which depreciation will apply, and for a slightly higher premium, a "replacement as new" insurance may be obtained from most insurers. Although most policies deal with claims for clothing and household linen on an indemnity basis, everything else is replaced without deductions.

Extensions to the household contents policy, for which an additional premium is not charged, include some cover in respect of property temporarily removed (for example, property taken by members of the family to places of employment) and loss or damage during removal of the home.

Household insurances may have sums insured in respect of buildings and contents separately, and each rated differently. There are insurances without a sum insured for contents and a premium based on the sum insured for the buildings. In addition policies are available without sums insured. Almost every insurer has a minimum premium although some offer special insurances for the elderly in which a low sum insured is available.

Prospectuses are available from most insurers and careful comparison will help a proposer to decide which one is most suitable for his or her requirements.

CHAPTER 4

The Insurance Contract

An insurance policy is a contract similar to any other commercial contract. There are, however, a few differences which will be examined in the course of this chapter.

As in all contracts there is an offer (sometimes from the insurer and at others from the insured). All contracts not under seal require consideration for them to be valid. In insurance that consideration is the payment, or the promise of payment, of the premium.

In general insurance (that is insurance other than life and marine insurance) the insurers issue a prospectus, which has a similar effect to a shopkeeper putting his or her wares in the shop window. An interested prospective insured supplies information on a proposal form which may be considered as an offer in law. The insurer may not accept but make a counter offer which the insured may accept or reject. The proposer accepts by paying the premium. If the insurance is arranged through an intermediary the same result is achieved.

In life insurance the proposer supplies relevant details on a proposal form, submits to a medical examination, if requested, and eventually (if all is well) receives an offer of insurance which may or may not be subject to terms. Unfortunately the document sent to him or her is called an "acceptance letter". Once again, acceptance of the offer is by payment of the premium.

Utmost good faith

One difference from other commercial contracts is immediately apparent. In all commercial contracts it is essential that there is an absence of fraud or fraudulent intent. A seller has no duty in contract to point out defects in the goods being offered for sale. There now exists a mass of consumer law to vary this simple situation. However, as far as the law of contract is concerned, there is no change.

In insurance contracts the duty goes beyond that simple requirement. Generally, only one person knows all the facts relating to the object to be insured. That person is the proposer who has a duty to divulge all the defects that he or she knows of in that object. This is known as utmost good faith (the Latin term is *uberrimae fidei*).

If it is a house that is to be insured the insurers would want to know about the materials used in its construction. If it is a motor insurance then there is the age of the car or the driver and his or her previous driving record. In insuring an item of jewellery insurers would need to know its age and value, about any previous claims and where it is kept.

As the law stands at present an insured also has a duty to provide other information not specifically asked about in the proposal form, provided it is relevant. This introduces a difficulty because a proposer must decide on the relevance of facts not asked. Examples of this could relate to criminal convictions. If a proposer failed to disclose all material facts then non-disclosure has taken place and there may not be a legal contract in existence.

The duty of disclosure exists during the negotiations leading up to the contract. Once the contract is in existence any changes may not invalidate the insurance. Insurances, other than life insurance, are renewable annually (technically the renewal is, in fact, a fresh contract) and any changes must be notified before renewal. Insurers may refuse renewal, offer amended terms or accept at normal terms. In most cases insurers also insert a policy condition requiring changes to be notified. The insurer again has the right to reconsider the contract. In some contracts insurers retain the right to cancel after giving seven days' notice in writing and refunding the unexpired premium.

In the case of life insurance, once the policy is in force and all material facts have been disclosed, the insurers cannot revise their terms or cancel the contract. Renewal does not affect the contract which is in existence for an agreed period of years or until death.

Example

Graham worked as an electrician with a film company. His job kept him moving from location to location. He was also disabled as he had a deformed right arm and his vehicle had been adjusted accordingly. When he proposed for insurance on his van he answered the question asking if he had any disabilities by writing "no". He also described himself simply as an "electrician".

After working 30 hours on location he was travelling through London, in the early hours of the morning to prepare at another location, when he fell asleep and his van veered across the road and struck an oncoming car.

The insurers' solicitors obtained a full statement of facts from him in order to defend a claim against him. However, after a copy of the statement had been sent to the insurers he was refused an indemnity. The insurers considered that he had not provided an accurate description of his job as well as failing to divulge his disability.

In this case the insurers were legally bound to indemnify him in respect of his third party liability by virtue of the requirements of the Road Traffic Acts. Any third party payment made could be claimed back from him but, in practice, insurers have little success in obtaining reimbursement in these circumstances.

Insurable interest

To insure any person or object one must have what is known as "insurable interest" in the subject of the insurance. The owner of whatever is to be insured may insure it at any time. Thus one can insure one's home, factory, car, jewellery and so on. It is also permissible to insure against the possibility that one may incur a legal liability or to insure one's own life and that of a spouse.

In each of the instances listed above the individual's right to insure is based on the fact that he or she would suffer a loss in the absence of insurance. No loss is suffered if someone else loses a valuable ring or is killed in an accident. Even if one has a moral duty, to a relative or friend for example, it is not insurable.

There are occasions when people have property in their possession which does not belong to them. They could have borrowed it or be looking after it for the owner (with or without payment). In these cases they acquire an insurable interest and can, therefore, effect insurance. The owner also retains their insurable interest.

Examples of non-owners insuring are repairers of cars, watches, televisions and shoes. Cleaners and dyers have an insurable interest, as have hotel proprietors (in certain circumstances). Carriers and owners of furniture depositories also have an insurable interest. Car park operators, too, have an interest. Even if it is believed that there is no legal liability in law, or effective disclaimers exist, insurance may still be effected and insurable interest may still exist.

Indemnity

Except for insurance on the human body or on human life all insurances are contracts of indemnity. This means that the intention of the insurance is to place the insured in the same (or as close as possible to the same) position after a loss as he or she was in before that loss occurred. The relationship between indemnity and insurable interest is obvious here. Unless insurable interest exists there can be no loss and, therefore, no idemnity.

Claims made for damage to property (houses, shops, factories or offices) will be settled on the basis of the actual cost of repairs necessitated by the insured incident. Subject to the sum insured being sufficient, insurers will pay the costs, although they are entitled to deduct the costs of any improvements made. If they are dealing with loss of goods then they are entitled to consider depreciation in order to reach the claims value. In many cases private house insurances are based on "new for old" rather than strict indemnity basis.

Where the loss involves stock the basis of settlement is the invoice price, although in some cases, goods may be worth less than the invoice price as a result of fashion changes.

Life insurance and personal accident insurance cannot be dealt with on an indemnity basis. No one can value a life or limb. Instead the insured decides on the sum to be insured at inception of the contract and that amount is paid if the loss insured against occurs. Thus a life insurance policy has a fixed sum insured (plus, perhaps, profit bonuses). Insurers will not restrict the sum insured subject to being satisfied that the proposer can afford the premium. If the sum insured appears to be far in excess of the proposer's station they might well be suspicious. For example, if a working man seeks a million pounds' life insurance, the reason may be intended suicide, although few people plan such an event far in advance.

If weekly benefits are involved, as in personal accident or continuous disability insurance, then insurers will restrict those benefits to a percentage of the proposer's weekly income. Once again it must not be assumed that insurers believe that people suffer self-inflicted injuries but they are concerned that benefits are not sufficiently inflated as to discourage the fit from an early return to work.

In some cases it is difficult for an insurer to determine if they are liable for indemnity under their insurance. To avoid harshness they will make a payment after declaring that there is no liability under the insurance. Such payments are called "ex gratia" payments. Insurers find that the insured will understand if prompt decisions are made and implemented. When an offer of an "ex gratia" payment is made after considerable investigation and delay insureds are apt to consider that insurers are attempting to avoid an indemnity.

Average

When faced with a claim, insurers may wish to be satisfied that full insurance exists. In the absence of full insurance they would be receiving less premium than they are entitled to. At the same time there would be unfairness against those who pay the full premium for their insurance. If they were satisfied that substantial under insurance existed then the claims payment would be reduced in proportion. This is known as "average".

Example

Thompson insured his stock for £40,000. Following a fire at his premises the insurers appointed an independent adjuster who reported that he had agreed the loss with the insured at £3500 and the cause of the fire as an insured peril. He also reported that a stock check had revealed that the actual stock at the time of the loss was £100,000.

The policy conditions included an average clause so that his settlement calculation was as follows:

Actual stock	£100,000	Loss	£3500
Sum insured	£40,000		

$$\frac{40,000 \times 3500}{100,000} = £1400$$

The practical effect is that the insured is treated as his or her own insurer for that part of the stock which was not insured. In the absence of an average clause insurers sometimes insert a warranty of "full value" insurance. Failure to insure for full value would invalidate the policy. However, in practice, insurers offer a settlement based on average.

Contribution

All contracts are contracts of indemnity except for life and personal accident insurance. In spite of this fact situations occur in which the insured has knowingly or unknowingly effected more than one insurance on the same risk. The result is that the insurers involved share the loss.

Assuming the existence of full insurance, each insurer will pay according to the relationship between his or her sum insured and the total value at risk.

Example

Kate bought a flat some years ago for £20,000. The building society insured it for £20,000 and charged the premium to her. Some years later, when reviewing her insurances, she realised that the flat was worth £60,000 and insured through another insurer for £40,000. A small fire took place damaging some of her property. She claimed £1000 from the new insurers and disclosed the existence of another policy.

The insurers agreed settlement as follows:

Insurer A paid $\dfrac{20,000 \times 1000}{60,000} = \text{£}333$

Insurer B paid $\dfrac{40,000 \times 1000}{60,000} = \text{£}667$

Total paid $= \text{£}1000$

Subrogation

After an accident an insured may have the option of claiming his or her losses against both the offending party or from his or her own insurers. Under a contract of indemnity he or she cannot do both. Where the contract is not one of indemnity it is possible to claim both under the insurance and against an offending party. As an example, if the holder of a life insurance or personal accident policy is killed as a result of the negligence of a third party the fact that insurers pay their liability under the insurance does not affect a claim made on behalf of the deceased's estate against the third party. Similarly, the victim of a road accident who receives payment under a personal accident insurance is not prevented from taking action against the culprit.

The holder of a contract of indemnity loses the right to recover his or her losses from the third party once his or her own insurers have indemnified him or her in full in respect of the losses. This is known as "subrogation". It is the right of an insurer having paid an indemnity in full to take over the rights of the insured. If necessary the insurer can use the insured's name and require his or her help (at the insurer's expense).

Although the right exists after settlement of the claim, policy conditions usually allow the insurers to use those rights before settling the claim.

Example

John stopped his car at the crossroads, looked carefully right and left for an opportunity to turn right. Suddenly he felt an impact and the car was thrown forward. After taking the details of the vehicle behind him he drove to a nearby garage. The car was quite safe on the road, he was told, once the rear lights had been temporarily repaired.

In due course an estimate for £750 arrived. John's broker explained that, although John had a comprehensive policy, if he wished to claim against the third party he could do so (although he must tell his own insurer). He could not also claim under his own policy. If he did claim under his own policy his insurers would try to recover from the third party motorist.

If his insurers were successful in recovering their loss John would not lose his "no claim discount". Most motor insurers have "knock for knock" agreements with each other. This means that they agree to waive their subrogation rights. The position of the no claim discount is not affected by the agreement. If a motorist does not have comprehensive insurance then he or she must prove the claim against the third party to the satisfaction of the third party's insurers.

One of the main advantages of comprehensive motor insurance is the fact that insurers will instruct repairs more rapidly. In many cases an insured is authorised to issue his or her own instructions in respect of minor damage. If a claim is made against third party insurers they will wish to inspect the damage (certainly they must be given a reasonable opportunity to do so). They will not wish to commit themselves until they have had a claim form from their insured and satisfied themselves that a claim against that insured exists. The work may have to be authorised and paid for before it is certain that the third party or his or her insurers will reimburse the damage and other losses (such as the hiring of a vehicle).

If the vehicle has to be taken off the road as a result of an accident, speed is the essence of the whole process. A comprehensive policy is obviously preferable.

Questions and answers

Q A friend of mine recently completed a proposal for insurance on his own life. A few days later he had a cold and visited his doctor who examined him and suggested that he saw a consultant as he suspected a minor heart condition. He received an acceptance letter from the insurers offering the insurance without a medical and sent them a cheque for the first premium. The following day he was seen by the consultant who confirmed a minor heart problem. Should he tell the insurers?

A Yes. Utmost good faith applies to insurance contracts. In the case of life insurance all material facts affecting the insurance must be disclosed in the period before the contract comes into existence. In this case until he had had an acceptance and paid his premium the contract was not yet complete. Had he gone to his doctor the day after he had paid the premium (and he had no reason to suspect a heart condition previously) it would not have been necessary to inform insurers.

Q I bought a house recently for £50,000 and, at the same time, borrowed £25,000 from a building society. They wished to insure the building but I refused and they allowed me to make my own arrangements. I insured it for £50,000 but they objected and asked for £60,000 insurance. In view of their limited financial interest in the transaction I refused. Can they insist?

A Until a few years ago building societies automatically insured properties on which they advanced money. Now most of them will allow borrowers to make their own arrangements which must be sufficient for rebuilding. They may charge a fee for this.

The value of their interest is irrelevant here because they obviously have an interest in the property being rebuilt after any insurable damage. The correct sum to insure for is the cost of rebuilding. This is based on a rate per square foot and varies slightly throughout the country. The Association of British Insurers produces a free booklet giving appropriate advice.

In addition to rebuilding costs there are also demolition costs and surveyors' and architects' fees. Additional costs, such as rebuilding brick walls and outbuildings, must also be allowed for. The market value of the property is not an indication because it is affected by land values. Most insurers offer an index linked policy.

Q George rented a disused building as a store. The owners warned him that it had been flooded three times in the previous ten years. The proposal from his insurers, however, only asked about his own previous claims history. He, therefore, did not feel it necessary to pass this information to them. A year later the premises were flooded and he submitted a claim. In reply to the adjuster's questions he admitted that he knew of the possibility of a flood but that he had not been asked by the insurers. The claim was refused on grounds of a breach of utmost good faith. Do you agree with this decision?

A One of the difficulties facing all who insure is knowing what is material and what is not. In this case it would seem that an insurer would be entitled to be told of the extra risk of flooding and would wish to have the opportunity to refuse the insurance or quote a higher premium. Some insurers would take the same action as

George's insurers did. Others, perhaps, might have dealt with the matter differently. If they felt that they would have accepted but at a higher premium had they been informed, they may be prepared to accept a back dated additional premium. In those circumstances they would pay the claim in full.

CHAPTER 5

The Insurance Market

Most insurances are arranged by intermediaries. Although using different titles to describe themselves, they all act on behalf of a proposer in finding suitable insurance cover. In many cases they advise the need for particular forms of insurance and, once a proposer agrees, endeavour to obtain cover from the insurers with whom they trade.

The insurers may be large proprietary companies transacting all classes of insurance (usually called "composites"), mutual companies or underwriters using the facilities at Lloyd's in London.

This chapter is intended to explain what is called the "insurance market" in brief non-technical terms.

Insurers

These accept insurance risks in return for payment of a premium. The origin of insurance is far back in ancient times when traders shared the risks of another trader who was sending a ship or its cargo to foreign lands. From the ancient civilisations it eventually settled in the Mediterranean and finally in London in the seventeenth century. Burial societies also existed in Roman times.

Some of the traders who took a share of the risk of a loss eventually specialised in this form of trading. They were called "underwriters" because they wrote their names on the original insurance document (called a "slip") below the details of the risk. During the eighteenth century they transacted most of their business in a coffee house in London owned by a man named Lloyd. Eventually they formed a committee and took over the coffee house which became a private organisation providing facilities for brokers to call on underwriters with details of insurance risks.

The practice continues at Lloyd's today with individuals accepting portions of insurance risks. Most of the individuals concerned do not have the knowledge to transact insurance themselves so they join groups of underwriters (called "syndicates") and employ a manager to run their business. The manager in turn employs someone to underwrite on behalf of the group. However, each member of the syndicate is only liable for his or her own share of any risk. This liability is unlimited. A member of Lloyd's must have considerable private assets, furnish security to be held in trust by Lloyd's, pay all premiums received into a fund from which claims are met and have his or her accounts independently audited.

In spite of the fact that Lloyd's underwriters are only responsible for their own share of a loss, Lloyd's maintains a central fund to which all underwriters contribute.

The individual underwriters are referred to as "names". Lloyd's is controlled by an elected committee and is self-regulating.

In 1720 a number of traders joined together and formed two groups, each of which was successful in obtaining a Royal Charter to form a company for the purpose of transacting insurance. In fact they also obtained a virtual monopoly as no other companies could be formed for the purpose. This did not affect individual underwriters.

One company was the London Assurance (now part of the Sun Alliance Group) and the other the Royal Exchange Assurance (now part of the Guardian Royal Exchange Group). After 1824 companies were allowed to be formed to transact insurance and some were set up by Act of Parliament. Subsequently new insurers were incorporated under the Companies Acts as limited liability companies.

Before the end of the sixteenth century some Government control existed in marine insurance and in 1870 life insurers were subject to legislation. Gradually legislation extended to all classes of insurance and, at the present time, insurers must have a minimum paid up capital based on the volume of business transacted and a minimum margin of solvency which must be in existence at all times. Control of insurers has steadily increased as a result of some dramatic failures and also because of our membership of the European Community. The controlling authority is the Department of Trade and Industry.

Mutual companies also exist in which the policyholders are the owners of the company and, as profits increase, receive the benefits of lower premiums and higher life insurance bonuses. Some of these have the word "mutual" in their title but others do not. In practice the differences in premiums and bonuses may be small and, as the larger proprietary insurers transact a greater volume of business, could be non-existent.

Some of the proprietary insurers are also empowered, under the Industrial Assurance and Friendly Societies Acts, to transact industrial life insurance ("home service insurance"). Premiums are collected weekly or monthly by collectors employed by the insurers. Many of these collectors are also able to transact ordinary life insurance and most of the classes of fire and accident insurance.

About the time of the Industrial Revolution friendly societies were formed to collect premiums to provide for burial. Many of these grew and some are today nationally known insurers. They also transact industrial life insurance by means of employed collectors.

In many trades mutual indemnity associations have developed as common pools into which members of particular trade associations could contribute and from which they could be reimbursed in the event of certain losses. The original objects were to reduce the costs of insurance by eliminating insurers' profits or because of the lack of suitable insurance available from the insurance market.

Eventually most mutual indemnity associations found the need to spread the risks beyond their own trade membership in order to provide greater financial stability. Many became proprietary companies and others became mutuals.

Intermediaries

In law all who act as intermediaries are agents. An agent acts on behalf of another to whom he or she has a duty of good faith. In insurance, most agents are agents of the proposer for part of the time and, except for brokers operating at Lloyd's, may act for the insurer at times too. This is a peculiarity of insurance agency as distinct from the laws of agency generally.

The agent is instructed in the first place by the proposer. Any information relevant to the proposal known to the agent must be divulged to the insurer. The agent can, if instructed by the proposer, complete the proposal on his or her behalf. In many cases agents receive insurance documents issued by insurers for passing on to their clients. As such they are responsible for payment of the premium or any other charges made by the insurer. They may, therefore, retain the documents on the insurer's behalf until those charges have been paid. At that time they are acting as agents of the insurer. The agent is paid by the insurer in the form of commissions (or, a term used by insurance brokers, "brokerage").

Although all intermediaries are agents in law, some are entitled to be called "brokers" and others use titles such as "consultant", "specialist" or "adviser".

An insurance broker must be registered in accordance with the Insurance Brokers (Registration) Act 1977. He or she is engaged in the business of insurance on a full time basis and holds the necessary professional qualifications. He or she will abide by the code of practice laid down for registration and have the minimum professional indemnity insurance needed. A broker will usually be a member of the British Insurance and Investment Brokers' Association.

The Financial Services Act 1986 affects the selling of life insurance and requires those engaged in selling it to be properly trained and able to confirm that the advice offered is the best suited to the needs of the client.

Those full time intermediaries who are not registered as insurance brokers may call themselves consultants or advisers. They are also affected by the Financial Services Act in the transaction of life insurance. In addition, since January 1989, the Association of British Insurers has instituted a code of practice for those engaged in general (that is, non-life) insurance who are not registered insurance brokers.

They must declare clearly whether they are independent or company agents. If they are independent then, whatever title they use, they are acting as brokers (but, as they are not recognised as such, cannot use the title). The requirement that they have professional indemnity insurance, which has been applied to insurance brokers, is also applied to the independent non-broker. A company agent is employed by a company who accepts responsibility for the way in which he or she operates. However, he or she may act for up to six companies who will share the responsibility.

One of the new legal requirements is that of disclosure of commission. This does not, at present, apply to "home service agents".

Home service insurance agents have been mentioned on a few occasions in this book. They are employed by an industrial life insurer or collecting friendly society. Their conditions of service vary but in general they are paid to collect premiums (and may get a commission on these collections). They are also paid for procuring new insurance business in the same way as other intermediaries.

Although legally described as collectors they do receive training and can offer a range of ordinary life insurances (as well as industrial life insurance) and the non-life insurance policies required by the householder and small business.

Reinsurance

Insurers have the same need as insureds to see that they have sufficient resources to meet unforeseen losses. In order that they may not be faced with losses that deplete their funds, insurers place part of some risks with other insurers (and accept parts of their risks in return) or with a specialist who is called a "reinsurer". The insured does not need to know of this nor is he or she party to a reinsurance contract. Insurers settle claims and, in due course, are reimbursed by reinsurers.

In most cases there are agreements (known as treaties) in force in which insurers automatically accept part of the risks accepted by other insurers. In return they receive a share of the premiums although in some classes of insurance reinsurers charge insurers a premium instead of accepting a share of the premium paid by the insured. Reinsurers pay an agreed proportion of all losses paid by insurers. Financial adjustments are made at agreed intervals.

In some cases insurers find it necessary to arrange for reinsurance for individual (usually very large) risks offered to them. This is called faultative reinsurance.

Associations

The Association of British Insurers

The ABI, as it is known throughout the insurance industry, was formed in 1985 to bring together the British Insurance Association and a number of other organisations representing the interests of insurers in fire, accident and life insurance. The members of the ABI between them transact 90% of the insurance dealt with by British insurers.

The ABI assists individuals and businesses by providing information about insurance and by giving advice on loss prevention through its educational activities. It also assists the public in disputes with insurers.

Insureds who feel aggrieved at particular situations that affect them should endeavour to communicate with an official of the insurer at the highest level. If they are dealing with local officials they should write to the head office of the company. If this fails to solve the problem then they should approach the Consumer Information Department of the ABI at Aldermary House, Queen Street, London EC4N 1TT (telephone 01-248 4477). The ABI may suggest an approach to the Insurance Ombudsman Bureau to which most insurers, including Lloyd's underwriters, belong. The Insurance Ombudsman Bureau (IOB) is at 31 Southampton Row, London WC1B 5HJ (telephone 01-242 8613).

Complaints referred to the Bureau have included refusal to pay a claim or paying insufficient (in the claimant's opinion) and delays in settlement. Complaints about intermediaries and surrender value calculations of life insurances cannot be dealt with by the Bureau.

If an insured continues to be dissatisfied he or she can take the matter through the courts.

The ABI publishes a number of very useful leaflets on insurance, safety and security. All of these are free. Application should be made to the local offices whose addresses are in *Useful Addresses*.

The British Insurance and Investment Brokers' Association

This is the professional organisation representing insurance brokers and those advising the public on investments. Those of its members transacting life insurance business carry professional indemnity insurance and are registered insurance brokers.

The Loss Prevention Council

This is an independent body replacing four organisations concerned with fire insurance and fire protection. The matters dealt with include fire protection, building construction and fire fighting.

Proposal forms

Except for very large industrial fire insurances, the information an insurer needs about the risk being offered to him or her is provided on a proposal form. The insurer selects those questions to which he or she requires an answer and prints them on a form for the proposer to complete. Although the proposer is under a duty to divulge all facts material to the risk it is intended that the form will reduce the need for either party to become involved in further enquiries. There is a difference in life insurance because further enquiries may need to be made to a medical attendant.

For simplicity the form is set out as a questionnaire and the basic information the insurer requires in order to consider acceptance should be available from a perusal of the answers given. Even if the insurer has doubts about acceptance (and the issue of a proposal form does not bind him or her) the proposal form is a convenient way of obtaining answers to the questions that arise before acceptance on any terms could be considered.

Insurers ask certain basic questions on all proposal forms. These include the name and address (and the address of the premises involved if different), the trade or occupation of the proposer, his or her age (if relevant as in life and personal accident insurance or motor insurance), details of the risk (if it is a shop, factory or garage, for example), the sum insured and previous claims or losses. Different classes of insurance involve different questions and separate forms are produced.

Until very recently any misstatement on a proposal form or in reply to a question could invalidate the insurance. This applied whether the misstatement concerned was in any way relevant to the loss or not. Insurers now have a voluntary code of conduct (the statements of practice are published by the Association of British Insurers) which restricts the strict application of the legal position. In effect, any misstatement made must be proved to be relevant to the loss in order to make the contract invalid in respect of that particular claim.

A proposal for a shopkeeper's insurance asks, in addition to the general questions listed above, about the contents. If there is a stock of tobacco and cigarettes or wines and spirits, insurers would wish to know the value. Certain other types of stock such as video tapes or jewellery could require separate enquiries.

If there is a safe in use insurers would want to have details of it.

Where cover is to include glass details would be needed, other than for plain glass. If work is carried out away from the premises details must be provided. If all risks cover is required, the insurers will wish to have a list of items and values.

At the end of each proposal form is a declaration for signature. For simplicity it is usual for the form to have a list of statements.

Example

The declaration below is an example of those used in shop-keepers' insurances. However, there are variations in practice and some more simplified forms of declaration may be found.

Declaration
The sums stated are the full value of the property in each case.
The only trade carried out in the premises is as stated above.
No inflammable liquids are stored on the premises.
The premises are built of brick, stone or concrete and roofed with slates, tiles, metal, asbestos or concrete. They are in a good state of repair and will be so maintained.
The area is normally free from flooding.
Power driven machinery is not used on the premises.
Full stock records will be kept and the accounts professionally audited.
   All persons proposed for personal accident insurance are in good health without physical or mental infirmities.
All security devices will be in operation when the premises are closed for business.
No insurer has ever declined a proposal, terminated an insurance or imposed special terms.
I declare that all the information given on this form whether in my own handwriting or written on my behalf is true in every respect. No material fact has been withheld. I agree to accept an insurance in the Company's normal form of contract for this class of insurance.

Signature........................   Date...................

The final statement should be looked at very carefully. If any doubts exist a full disclosure should be made. If the proposal form itself does not leave sufficient space for a full answer and one appears essential, then these facts should be written on the other side of the form or added on a separate sheet and referred to in the answer. It is always a good idea to retain a copy of the information provided in the proposal form. It should be noted that many insurers dispense with detailed declarations and, in some cases, especially in connection with fire and extra perils insurance, may not have a declaration at all.

There are two important facts to be brought to the insurer's attention by the proposer. One has already been dealt with: that is the question of full disclosure of material facts. The other is the proposer's need to make perfectly sure that the insurer understands exactly what is to be covered. If, for example, at certain times of the year the cash limit is particularly high, then a note explaining this would ensure full cover. It is fatal to assume that insurers are aware of the particular problems or special situations in the proposer's trade.

Surveys

In most cases insurers will arrange for the premises to be surveyed. The surveyors will prepare a plan for the underwriter showing the nature of the risks involved. They will probably advise on the rate of premium to be applied and comment on the sum insured stated by the proposer. He or she may make suggestions for improving the risk and, in this connection, it is advantageous if a senior member of the firm is available for discussion as much correspondence — and its attendant misunderstandings — can be avoided. They may also impose compulsory requirements — such as intruder alarms. The surveyors may also point out certain features which, if improved, will result in a saving of premium, or, at the same time, may insist on certain improvements. It must be obvious that any improvements they suggest or wish to apply are as much in the interests of the business as of the insurer.

It is advantageous to call on surveyors' services as early as possible if new premises are in the process of being built, altered or about to be occupied. It is more difficult and costly to make changes at a late stage. Their services are free and should be used to the full.

In small businesses insurers may be satisfied with the opinion of their local representative for the area. These representatives are usually called "inspectors". Unfortunately this archaic title does not explain what they do. In brief, the inspectors are the insurers' local representatives and their physical contacts with their agents. They are trained in the requirements of insurance surveying and are well aware of the underwriters' requirements. The inspectors are not specialists (in fact they are often called "maids of all work") but can call on help and advice if it is required.

For very large risks insurers will either have, or can call upon, specialist surveyors in fire, theft and liability insurance. In some areas of the country the fire surveyor, who is trained in the problems of different building materials, manufacturing processes and fire precautions, may also be specially trained in particular industries concentrated in the area.

Theft surveyors will look at the premises from the point of view of a thief. The questions they will ask themselves are related to the attractiveness of the stock and the size and weight of individual items or packages. If the stock is attractive and expensive then special precautions are essential. Examples are barring windows and skylights and reinforcing doors. They will want to minimise the number of exits in daily use (other exits may need special attention so that they can be used as fire exits) and have only one door of "final exit". A door of final exit cannot be bolted on the inside as other doors and windows can. This is the door through which the person responsible for locking the premises leaves. It usually requires strong hinges, a mortice lock, and it should also be reinforced.

In many cases today the installation of an intruder alarm is regarded as essential. A surveyor may suggest the installation of a safe. In some cases the latter may be suggested by the fire surveyor as a protection for books and certain files. If it is required to protect against theft then, according to the value of the items concerned, a thief resistant safe may become necessary. More details of security precautions may be found in the next chapter.

Policy forms

Insurers issue a policy document so that the terms of the agreement entered into between the insured and the insurer are clear and unambiguous. The proposer agrees to accept a policy in the insurer's usual form for the class of risk. He or she is entitled to ask to see a specimen copy of the form which will eventually be provided. Unfortunately few do (this may show confidence in the insurer or the agent) and, what is even worse, many do not even bother to read the policy when it does finally arrive. This is partly due to the fact that policyholders expect the policy to contain uninformative jargon and the proverbial "small print". Over the years many insurers have set out to improve the language used in their documents and others have even succeeded in receiving awards for the use of plain English in their documents.

The modern insurance policy is a standard document for the particular class of insurance, to which is added a schedule. The schedule is referred to in the policy and contains the specific details of the risk and the insured. Whereas the entire policy is printed, the schedule can be handwritten or typed, although it is very likely to be produced by computer.

The sections of a modern "scheduled" policy are:

(a) *Heading*

This is simply the name and address of the insurer for communication purposes.

(b) *Recital*

This explains that the policy, the schedule, the conditions, the exceptions and the endorsements form one contract. They are to be read together and any words used will have the same meaning wherever they appear.

The wording refers to the proposal form and the payment or agreement to pay the premium. Most policy forms contain the words " . . . a proposal which shall be the basis of the contract and deemed to be incorporated herein". At one time a copy of the proposal form was, in fact, attached to the policy but subsequently it was simply referred to in the wording used. The effect is to convert the proposer's declaration of truth into a warranty. Thus any breach, whether relevant to a loss or not, entitles the insurers to repudiate the contract.

The Association of British Insurers issued statements of practice relating to private insurances in 1985/6. The object of the statements was to relieve those who were applying for insurances in a private capacity from such an onerous duty as that detailed in the previous paragraph. Although the duty of disclosing all material facts truthfully still exists any breach must be relevant before insurers are enabled to repudiate the contract.

(c) *Operative*

The cover granted by the insurance is fully set out. In some insurances a few lines will suffice. In others, such as traders', householders' and motor comprehensive insurance, many pages of detail are necessary.

This is a very important section which the insured should read very carefully, comparing the details with the information stated in the prospectus. Any doubts should be taken up with the insurers or the agents. It is usually advisable to get written assurance if a particular section does not appear to be granting the cover required.

There are exceptions listed in this section. If the section is very detailed there may also be exceptions listed for each part and a set of "general exceptions" at the end of the section. These are very important and should be read carefully. In many cases a particular exception can be deleted for an additional premium.

(d) *Conditions*

Certain conditions are implied in common law and do not have to appear in writing. They are, firstly, that the insured has an insurable interest in the insurance (simply expressed this means that an individual cannot insure something that does not affect him or her financially. Thus you cannot insure your neighbour's life or his or her car). The second condition is of utmost good faith (declaring all known relevant facts). The third is that the object insured actually exists and the fourth that it can be identified (for example, a one pound coin could not be identified — they all look the same).

Insurers may print some of these conditions in their policies to remind policyholders. They will also add others that they feel are necessary. Some conditions add benefits — in a life insurance policy there may be information about the availability of a surrender value or non-cancellation (automatic action taken by insurers to prevent lapsing of the insurance due to non-payment). In most policies there will be details of the way in which a claim must be submitted and the insurer's procedure for dealing with claims. This is a very important condition which should be read carefully. It will stipulate the notice required of an occurrence. How an insured or insurer may cancel the contract (if applicable) will be explained here and also provision for arbitration in the event of a dispute.

(e) *Signature*
The policy will be signed in the way approved in the insurer's own rules.

(f) *Endorsements*
Sometimes there are amendments necessary to the wording of the policy (an example is the removal of an exception on payment of an additional premium). This is done by adding slips which are usually headed "endorsement" and often given a reference letter and/or number. Issuing a fresh policy each time there is a change, would increase the administration considerably.

Insurers seldom ask for the policy to be sent to them for the endorsement to be attached to the policy so that it is important for the insured to actually attach it as soon as it is received. The absence of an endorsement could affect the insured's judgement when considering the notification of a claim.

(g) *Warranties*
In some cases insurers wish to stipulate a particular course of action on the part of the insured. An example is: "The intruder alarm will be in operation at all times when the premises are closed for business". This is a warranty and any breach would invalidate the insurance, whether the breach is relevant or not. For example, strictly according to the legal position, failure to switch on the intruder alarm before leaving the premises would invalidate a combined business insurance even if the claim was in respect of fire.

In private insurances insurers have agreed not to avoid liability unless the breach is relevant to the claim (the Statements of Practice of the Association of British Insurers referred to above).

Renewal procedure

Some life insurances are purchased by payment of a lump sum and there are fire insurances which are in force for periods in excess of a year. In general, however, most insurances are renewed annually. Variations are for "short period" policies in force for less than a year and life insurances for which premiums are paid more often than annually (that is half-yearly, quarterly or monthly by banker's order or direct debit).

Unless insurers expressly state an intention, they do not have to send notifications of renewal to a policyholder. In practice the majority do send notices either to insureds or their agents. It is advisable, in any event, for an insured to keep a record of dates (in the business diary preferably) should a renewal date be overlooked by the insurers. It is the policyholder's responsibility to renew.

In the case of life insurances, renewal simply means sending the appropriate premium within the days of grace. Insurers allow "days of grace", which are periods of time varying from 14 days to 1 month after the renewal date during which they consider the insurance effective should the premium be paid within that time.

In general insurance renewal is legally regarded as a fresh contract. In addition to premium payment, policyholders have a duty to notify changes which have taken place, and which affect the insurance, since the previous renewal.

Most non-life insurances have a policy condition which requires notification of changes affecting the insurance as soon as they occur. Examples are, changes of address, type of trade, type of stock, or physical alterations in the premises.

As these are conditions (and not warranties) the breaches must be material if the insurer is to consider repudiating a claim.

No "days of grace" are allowed in motor insurance but it is usual to attach an insurance certificate to a renewal notice. Provided the notice has been received by the policyholder the certificate allows a period of insurance to comply with the Road Traffic Act. This cover, generally of 15 days, enables the vehicle to be used on a road by providing the necessary third party insurance cover. This cover is not conditional on the insured renewing the insurance. It is only invalidated by the existence of another motor insurance. Insurers may honour the entire insurance contract if they regard the delay in payment as an oversight or administrative error.

This difference between motor insurance, and other insurances, should be noted. Motor insurance policies also have a cancellation condition, as most other general insurances, but require the return of the annual "certificate of insurance" issued at inception of the policy and at renewal. If this document is not returned to the insurers within seven days they have the right to take legal action for its return. In this case the "permanent" certificate is referred to as it is usual in motor insurance for agents to issue a temporary certificate (called a "cover note") until the permanent document is produced. The cover note must be timed and dated and it is illegal to show a date and time prior to issue. Further cover notes may be required until the certificate of insurance is ready for delivery.

Premium payments

Life insurance premiums may be paid in a lump sum or annually. Most insurers also accept instalments of the annual premium for a small extra payment, which could be 2½% to 5%. Instalments could be paid half-yearly or quarterly. An extra charge may also apply in respect of monthly instalments which must be paid by bankers' order or direct debit. Many insurers encourage this convenient form of payment by quoting a monthly premium with no discount offered for annual payments.

In the event of death during an insurance year the balance of that year's premium is deducted from the sum insured. Some insurers quote a "true" quarterly or monthly premium and charge an additional, say, 5%. These are not instalments of the annual premium and no further sum is due if death takes place during an insurance year. In fact many insurers only quote true, and not instalment, premiums.

In the case of general insurances, some intermediaries can arrange for payment by instalments or accept the major credit cards. Some insurers are prepared to accept premiums spread over five months without additional charge. Others have various credit schemes allowing for payments spread over twelve months with interest at, or slightly below, the market rate.

Questions and answers

Q The local garage telephoned last Saturday morning to say that the new car ordered for my wife had arrived. I rang my insurance company about a motor insurance policy for her. The girl I spoke to said it "would be alright" if my wife wanted to collect the car as a cover note would be posted immediately. On the way home with the car she was stopped by a police car who checked her documents and gave her a slip to take with the insurance certificate to a police station.

The cover note did not arrive in the post on Monday morning and at 11 o'clock my wife rang the insurance company who sent her a cover note. When it arrived we found that it was timed and dated from 11.40 am Monday. Although I explained the situation they refused to issue one from Saturday. They said they did not know who I spoke to but, in any case, no cover note had been prepared for my wife and they could not now issue one dated earlier.

A Legally your wife was wrong in driving the car on a road before she had an insurance certificate (or cover note) in her possession. Had the insurers completed the cover note as arranged she would have been able to produce it at the police station. It has generally been assumed that if the cover note is in the post it is operative from the time of posting. However, it sometimes happens that cover notes are not completed exactly when requested. For example, if a clerk has ten to write, the last one could be dated an hour later — perhaps after the time the enquirer had started using the car. It is illegal to backdate a cover note.

The duty is on the user of a vehicle to ensure that he (or she) has third party insurance before taking it on to a road. It is much safer to arrange for the necessary cover early and obtain the document before putting the vehicle on the road.

Q I have taken over a small workshop on a nearby farm and will be engaged in panel beating and repainting private cars. I have insured my stock and I have a motor traders' insurance, but my insurance adviser is trying to persuade me to insure customers' cars against fire and explosion. I accept no liability for cars on my premises and, anyway, the customer has them insured. What do you advise?

A I feel that it is important to you to insure in respect of your legal liability to the owners of the cars brought to you for repair. Firstly, the customer may only have third party insurance and would look to you for reimbursement if his or her car was lost or damaged as a result of a fire whilst it was in your possession. Secondly, the motor trade policy would not cover this particular risk. Thirdly, the exclusion clause in the contract with your customer or notices displayed, even if effective, may be overridden by an allegation of negligence on the part of you or your employees. In law, as a bailee, you have special responsibilities towards your customers' property. Therefore any exclusion clause could be invalid under the Unfair Contract Terms Act 1977.

Even a fire caused by vandals may be held to have been avoidable had you taken extra precautions.

The loss of one car could be expensive for you but imagine a fire followed by an explosion destroying perhaps ten cars! If you are near to the premises of others you should also have cover for possible damage to their property.

Q I left my car outside the house a few weeks ago and my neighbour reversed into it. He paid for the repair as it was only £50. As I have a comprehensive motor policy I sent a claim form to my insurers. They have now written to say that my neighbour has paid for the damage and I cannot claim under the policy. I don't understand that because I pay them for insurance — why won't they pay up?

A Motor insurance policies, like all other insurances, except for life and personal accident, are contracts of indemnity. That is, they promise to put you as near as possible in the same financial position after a loss as you were in before the loss. In this case you have suffered no loss as your neighbour has, quite rightly, paid for the repairs.

If you wished you could have claimed the cost of repairs from your insurer who would be subrogated to your rights (that is, take over your rights against your neighbour) and claim the costs back from your neighbour. Your neighbour could, of course, ask his insurers to pay.

Q I have a motor policy which is for third party only. I sent a completed claim form to my insurers after an accident in which I sustained over £400 in damage to my car. I did not hear from them again so I telephoned and they said that I would have to contact the other party, or his insurers, if I wanted to claim for my own damages. They told me that they had a "knock for knock" agreement with the other insurer and they had, therefore, filed their papers. Is this correct?

A Yes, I am afraid so. The "knock for knock" provides that each insurer will pay his own insured's damage, less any excess applicable. In your case as you only had third party insurance your insurer did well out of the agreement and had no one to pay (unless the other person was third party only or had an excess and can prove a claim against you). The object of the agreement is to avoid the need for costly correspondence and argument over liability and it would defeat that intention if they got involved to assist you.

As you are not insured for your own damage you must send an estimate to the other party notifying him that you hold him responsible or ask your insurers for the name and policy number of the other party's insurers and write direct to them. It will probably be a long haul and, unless you have good independent evidence, a difficult one. You will benefit from the use of a solicitor unless you belong to the AA, RAC or other organisation offering legal assistance. There are many schemes available: some offer a car hire and breakdown recovery as well as a service to recover your uninsured losses. Your insurance agent or broker may offer this service for a fee.

Q I read in the local paper recently about a man who was prosecuted for driving without insurance because his insurers refused to idemnify him. The reason they gave was that he had not told them that he had been disqualified from driving for one year and had only just got his licence back. The reporter said that the insurer's action is callous in the extreme because a passenger was very seriously injured and will get no compensation. Is there no way he can be helped?

A Motor insurers who refuse an indemnity to their insured as a result of non-disclosure must pay a valid third party claim. So the injured passenger claim will be paid in the usual way. The Act gives the insurer the right to claim back all payments and costs from the policy-holder. This right is usually of no value at all. Where there is no insurance at all the Motor Insurers' Bureau (with funds contributed to by all motor insurers) will pay the claim as if it is against them. These contributions seriously affect motor insurance premiums.

Q Last July my next door neighbour's home was broken into and his television and video recorder stolen. He called the police. The thief was quickly found and he still had the television but the video had been sold. In court he mentioned that he knew my neighbour because they had been in prison together when my neighbour was serving a five year sentence for burglary. Now my neighbour's insurers have refused to pay the claim because he did not tell them about his record. As there is no question asking about it on the proposal form I can't see how they can get away with it.

A This is a problem for a proposer and one that a Law Reform Committee has been looking at. The question is how does a proposer know what an insurer regards as material? A proposer must divulge all material facts. The fact that he has been in prison for theft is material to a proposal for theft insurance but also tells insurers something about the character of the proposer. That, too, is vital in all insurances.

CHAPTER 6

Safety, Security and Fire Protection

Security against theft

In any business security is vital but there is no such thing as perfect security. What the business person must do is to consider the premises from the point of view of a thief and then plan to make his or her activities difficult. The more difficult the entry the greater the chance that the thief will be disturbed or caught.

Quite obviously a potential intruder is going to be deterred by impressive protections. He or she will be encouraged to seek other premises rather than spend the time necessary to enter a fortress. Naturally there must be a relationship between the security installed and the risk presented. The greengrocer will not wish to consider the protections that a jeweller wants installed.

This is a good time to remind readers of the services of their insurers. Insurers employ specialists in intruder security (many are still known by the old title of "burglary surveyor"). The services of these specialists are free. There may also be valuable discounts to be obtained from the insurer by following their surveyor's advice. Free advice is also available from the crime prevention officer at the local police station.

It must also be borne in mind that vandalism and arson can take place without penetrating security. A householder who had a security grille installed died in a fire caused by petrol being poured through the letter box and ignited.

The main considerations involved are:

(a) *The type of business*
This is of great importance. Insurers are very well aware of the use to which premises are put in the various trades. In fact,

they will have statistical information on which to base their judgement and the advice they can give their policyholders.

(b) *The attractiveness of the goods carried and the machinery and equipment used*

Value and portability affect the attractiveness of the goods and equipment and the ease of disposal is relevant. The one item that complies with all three criteria is cash. Reading down the list we can note jewellery, cigarettes, wines and spirits, small electronic office machines and portable tools. Although one could say that furniture, building materials and grocery would be very low on the list, someone will steal them. Even fairly large mobile plant can "disappear" from a building site.

(c) *Construction*

Premises built of brick or concrete and roofed with slates, concrete or tiles are safer to house property in than buildings made of timber, asbestos sheets or corrugated iron.

(d) *Unoccupied premises*

If the premises are unoccupied for long periods by day or night it is possible for thieves to enter and work at their leisure. The opposite situation is in premises in which staff are present throughout the day with responsible persons on the premises outside business hours. Where possible on-site security guards controlling entry to and exit from the premises (this can deter pilfering) and an irregular patrol offer good security. Visits by outside security guards, although useful, are only of limited value. The vandal or arsonist can be a real problem at an isolated building unoccupied for very long periods, especially at weekends. There are special regulations concerning the use of guard dogs and, although their use by patrols is advantageous, the animals cannot be left unattended.

(e) *Ease of access to premises*

If vehicles can be driven close to premises or directly on to sites quantities of goods can be removed rapidly. In some cases fork lifts are available nearby to help with the loading of goods! Otherwise, ease of entry from footpaths can also be a factor.

Occupants must consider the possible use of stairways, both

internal and external, as well as flat roofs leading to adjoining premises. This is one area where the occupier must try to visualise all possible ways in which property can be removed. Single storey roofs assist access to first floor windows which must be protected to the same standard as ground floor ones.

(f) *Protections*

(i) Fencing should be strong. Chain link fencing to BS 1722: Part 10 is preferable to brick walls or wooden fences. The thief must not be protected from view once on the premises. Fences should be 2.4 metres high with proper straining wires and anchoring. Gates must not be able to be lifted off their hinges and they should be secured with good locking bars and strong close shackle padlocks.

(ii) Doors must be strong and reinforced if necessary by steel sheets. The frame must be properly attached to the walls. Strong hinges with hinge bolts should be used. Locks should be mortice deadlocks conforming to BS 3621 as a minimum. Rimlocks should not be used on a door of final exit. The weakest situation is that of the door with rimlocks and glass panels. The thief simply breaks the glass and turns the lock from the inside. The deadlock can only be opened with a key from either inside or outside.

This has other advantages. When the thief is leaving the premises he or she will be carrying booty. If it is not possible to open locked doors or windows he or she must leave the same way as he or she entered — possibly through a broken window, clambering over the broken glass. The thief will take these factors into consideration when deciding how much he or she can carry away.

(iii) Key security is important. One person must be responsible for the keys. That person must check the building and fences daily. Keys should not be left in locks or hung on a board clearly labelled with room or building numbers. A suitable colour code should be used on keys. The keys should be kept in a locked cupboard.

It is possible to use locks with key registration to prevent the dishonest copying of keys.

(iv) Window bars and/or mesh should be fitted to windows. Doors not required could be bricked up. The minimum number of doors should be in regular use. This is difficult in a shop as other considerations may dictate differently. In other risks it should be possible to restrict entry to one security controlled door. Any other doors may need to be used as emergency exits and the advice of the local fire brigade is valuable here.

(v) Shopfronts may need protecting by the use of removable grilles or roller shutters. Some shops may benefit from the use of permanent grilles to protect against "smash and grab" type attacks.

(g) *Lighting*

Internal lighting used outside normal business hours can give the impression of occupation and cause a possible intruder to stop and consider the risks involved in attempting an unauthorised entry. There are a variety of devices available which can operate lighting at regular or irregular intervals to reinforce the impression of occupation.

Good outside lighting is a powerful deterrent as no thief wishes to be working in full view of other people. Lighting is also available which can operate automatically when anyone approaches within defined distances from it.

(h) *Safes*

If money, important documents or valuables are to be left on the premises a thief resistant safe (as distinct from a fire proof one) is essential. The safe should be securely fixed to the building. Insurers may specify the type to be used as a minimum. As with door keys, someone must hold the safe keys or combination code. These must not be left on the premises outside normal business hours and insurers will usually impose a warranty on the insurance policy accordingly. Spare keys or copies of the combination code should be deposited at the bank.

(i) *Intruder alarms*

The discussions that take place here are between those who believe that an alarm should be used to scare off intruders and those who feel that they ought quietly to summon the police. The latter theory is based on the belief that putting thieves out of business is preferable to the community than just chasing them away to look for easier targets.

It is, of course, possible to install alarms that sound an audible warning as well as summon the police.

All alarms should be installed and maintained to the requirements of BS 4737. Most insurers insist that installation and maintenance is carried out by members of the National Supervisory Council for Intruder Alarms (their address can be found under *Useful Addresses* at the end of the book).

It is not possible to specify the type of detector to use. The circumstances vary so that only a survey report from a qualified installer or the insurer's surveyor will be able to supply the essential individual advice. Some detectors operate when doors or windows are opened, others can detect a presence in a room.

General security arrangements

There are a number of actions which should be taken to reduce the risk of loss:

(a) Cash should be kept under lock and key (except for tills in constant use which should be carefully sited to prevent someone stealing from them when opened).

(b) The practice of leaving money in unlocked cash boxes or drawers must be stopped.

(c) Female staff should be encouraged to stow handbags away as they are attractive to unauthorised persons who may be passing.

(d) Trusted and able bodied persons should be used for taking money to banks. Insurers will advise on procedures.

(e) Take great care in checking references or testimonials when appointing staff.

(f) Mark portable items of value with the post code, using engraving or, if not possible, ultra-violet markers.

(g) Make sure vehicles are locked each time they are left unattended and that coats, briefcases or parcels are stowed in the locked boot.

Fire and arson protection

Fire is the major hazard facing any business. Fire insurance premiums are based on the factors which, in the insurer's opinion, can start and spread fire. The fire risk in a building is generally that of the most hazardous business being carried on in that building.

The trade processes may be a potential source of fire hazard if, for example, they involve highly flammable waste, liquids or dust. The important features are the combustibility of the raw materials, packaging and finished goods. In particular, the method of storage plays a big part. If any of the materials are highly combustible they can ignite easily and assist in the rapid spread of fire.

Other features are:

(a) Construction — the materials used in the ceilings and partitions. These should not be capable of increasing the risk and spread of fire. If there are fire-break walls and floors the risk is lessened and most insurers recognise this by charging a lower rate of premium.

(b) The term "housekeeping" is used to relate to the tidyness of the business which includes:

  (i) Fire safety. This must be the personal responsibility of the owner or delegated to a senior person in a larger firm. That person must make a final check of the entire premises at the end of the business day.

  (ii) Smoking. If this cannot be banned entirely then it should not be allowed in hazardous areas. Definite rules must be agreed.

  (iii) Combustible goods. These should be stored away from the main building, leaving only sufficient materials in the building for day to day use. This applies particularly to bulk flammable liquids. The outbuilding should be a sufficient distance from the main building to avoid the spread of fire if it should ignite. The door of the store should be securely locked against vandals.

  (iv) Any part of the building or any building that is not in use should be cleared of combustible materials and securely locked.

  (v) Combustible waste which must be cleared daily and kept at a safe distance from the building. In view of the possibility of it being used by arsonists it is advisable that care be taken to prevent easy access to it.

  (vi) Keeping a careful watch for unauthorised persons on the site and seeing that the person responsible for locking up at the end of the working day checks that no one has been left on the premises.

(c) A safe method of heating is essential whether from a central boiler or from local electric heaters carefully guarded and placed clear of combustible materials. In the case of electricity, great care must be taken to see that wiring is regularly checked and is not overloaded. Trailing wires and adapters must be avoided. Examinations of the wiring must be carried out regularly and at least every five years by a qualified electrician. In areas of greater hazard from flammable gases it will be necessary to install special switch gear.

An emergency main switch should be easily accessed and staff must be aware of its location.

Protection against weather and water damage

Bursting of water pipes, tanks and other apparatus can be protected against by efficient lagging. If possible premises or parts of premises not in use should have their water supply cut off and tanks and apparatus drained. If this is not possible care must be taken to provide a minimum of heating in inclement weather. A thermometer should be used to ensure that the air temperature does not fall below 4°C.

Equipment, especially ballcocks, should be inspected regularly. Stopcocks should be tested often and all employees should know where they are located.

Checks should be made of the condition of flat roofs to avoid leakage of rain water. Gutters should be cleared regularly and all downpipes checked.

If flooding is possible materials should be raised from the floor on blocks, bricks or pallets. In that type of situation the use of basements should be avoided. In other cases it is preferable to site machines away from the possibility of flooding or rain water leakage. The method of storage of goods will depend on its packaging and susceptibility to water damage.

Tall buildings should be protected against lightning in accordance with BS 326 (lightning conductors).

Accident prevention

Both common law and statute law require an employer to observe certain precautions. These include proper maintenance of floors, stairways and passageways (including the availability of adequate handrails), fencing of moving parts of machinery (including proper maintenance), correct training of employees and supervision of improvers.

An insurer's accident surveyor will have regard to the condition of floors, stairs, roofs, chimney stacks, forecourts, trap doors, cellar flaps, goods chutes, pavement lights, gratings, coal plates, areas, signs and flagstaffs. He or she will look closely at trade processes and the machinery in use and will also be concerned with stacking, storage facilities and methods, lifting appliances and the special considerations applying to particular trades and occupations.

The surveyor will advise on accident prevention and reduction as well as the use of effective disclaimer notices where appropriate.

His or her advice is especially valuable because, although those involved in the particular trades will have had experience of the type of incidents that can occur, the surveyor will be able to draw on his or her own experiences and those of colleagues nation wide. An experienced person walking the floor of the site can often spot dangerous situations that have not been visualised by even the most experienced manager.

Technical information on safety matters is available from the Industrial Safety Division of the Royal Society for the Prevention of Accidents whose services are often used by insurers.

Portable fire extinguishers

Even the smallest business unit requires some form of fire fighting equipment. The most generally used are suitable fire extinguishers backed up with buckets of water and sand or, in larger establishments, with hose reels.

Most business premises and hotels have a legal obligation, if they employ staff, under the Fire Precautions Act 1971 to provide suitable fire fighting equipment and maintain it. In many cases insurers stipulate the installation of specific equipment.

Extinguishers should comply with BS 5423 (some existing extinguishers that comply with earlier standards are acceptable) and be approved by the Fire Offices' Committee or be certified under the

British Approvals for Fire Equipment scheme. The Fire Protection Association will provide a list of Approved Portable Fire Extinguishers free on request. Enquiries should be addressed to them at the Loss Prevention Council (see under *Useful Addresses* at the back of this book).

Information is also available on the suitability, siting, inspection, testing and maintenance of extinguishers. Leaflets are obtainable on the use of fire extinguishers and films, videos, slides and posters to assist with fire safety training may be purchased from the Fire Protection Association.

Extinguishers should be sited as near as possible to exits or on staircase landings. They should be positioned no more than 30 metres from each other. In large undivided areas they should be located on escape routes. If there is a great deal of equipment it would be advantageous to locate it at one convenient point. If there are major flammable liquid and electrical equipment risks, extinguishing apparatus should be located as close as possible to these hazards. All equipment should be conspicuous.

Extinguishers should be provided in numbers and sizes as recommended by BS 5306. Tested extinguishers are marked with a number reflecting the size of the fire they can deal with and a letter A or B. Letter A indicates that they are suitable for use on a fire involving solid materials and letter B for liquids. Some extinguishers that are suitable for solids and liquids carry the letters A and B.

On a floor under 100 square metres a 9 litre water extinguisher would be a minimum requirement. Any type of extinguisher having a Class A rating — even a dry powder unit — would be suitable unless any special hazards exist.

The size and number of extinguishers to be used for flammable liquids varies according to the size of container in use. Special requirements exist for areas in which there is a risk of uncontrolled spillage.

Extinguishers marked as suitable for dealing with fires in electrical equipment should be sited close to the equipment.

A responsible person should inspect and check extinguishers monthly. An annual service by the manufacturers or service company should be carried out at least once a year.

Extinguishers are colour coded as follows:

Red   — These use water to cool down fires. They are suitable for most fires except those involving flammable liquids or live electrical apparatus.

Blue — Consist of dry powder and are suitable for all types of fires even if involving flammable liquids or electricity.

Cream — Designed for fires involving flammable liquids and contains foam. As it is not suitable for all liquids the manufacturer's instructions should be read.

Green — These are also suitable for use on fires involving flammable liquids and electrical apparatus. However, as they contain halon, they should not be used in confined spaces if there is a danger that the fumes may be inhaled.

Black — Also suitable for fires involving flammable liquids or electrical apparatus but, as they contain carbon dioxide, they should not be used in confined spaces if there is a risk of inhalation.

Basic instruction in fire fighting and the use of fire extinguishers is available from the fire service. It is essential that staff in a small unit know how to operate fire fighting equipment and in a larger one designated staff should have the necessary training. Although the manufacturer's instructions appear to be clear this may not be so in an emergency. Training can be valuable.

In a fire emergency the fire brigade must be called immediately. Delay can be dangerous. The fire service must be given the opportunity of attending the fire at an early stage.

If it is possible to switch off electricity and gas from a main point safely, this should be carried out. Someone must have the responsibility of calling the fire service. Unless the fire is very small immediate evacuation must be ordered. Attempts to extinguish the fire must be abandoned if life is in danger: there is a possibility of the exit being cut off or the fire may be growing in spite of attempts to extinguish it.

If there is a gas supply and it cannot be turned off or gas cylinders are present the area should be immediately evacuated. All doors and windows should be closed, if possible, before withdrawing.

Emergency lighting, especially if automatically operated in the event of the failure of the mains supply, can be valuable. Fire and smoke detection equipment should be installed and tested regularly.

It is important that staff are familiar with the sounds of the alarm in use and that they are trained in taking appropriate actions. Except where there are only a few staff, an assembly point should be designated in the event of an emergency and all staff must report to a senior member. This is particularly important if there are disabled persons in the building.

CHAPTER 7

Claims Procedure

The object of insurance is to provide for situations in which the insured suffers a loss. Policyholders do not see themselves as buying insurance but a facility that will pay for certain losses that will inevitably arise. The way in which a claim is dealt with adds value to the existing sale and introduces the possibility of cross selling. A policyholder who has received good service will feel a desire to recommend that insurer to his or her friends and colleagues. Much louder will be the sounds from the dissatisfied claimant who will transmit chapter and verse to anyone prepared to listen. Almost everyone in business has a dissatisfied customer. Unfortunately a claimant under an insurance policy is suffering a trauma. It may be the destruction of a factory, the loss of a spouse or a dent in the wing of a car. To the claimant, at that moment in time, a tragedy has struck. Everyone reacts in a different way to these incidents. All are upset and require the same careful consideration. What no one wants is unnecessary "red tape".

Not all claims are covered by the insurances held and it is a sad fact that many do not seek advice when insuring, receive poor advice or do not heed the advice given. Very often a proposer for insurance adopts the view that insurance is an additional expense which must be kept to a minimum. The agent's advice is considered as possible self-interest and, in fact, until agents and brokers charge fees instead of receiving commissions the doubt will always exist. This is not to say that there are agents who are more concerned with their own financial reward than the service that they are supposed to be giving.

Whilst it is true that everyone in business needs to look very carefully at the costs insurance must be looked at as an essential item and the need carefully assessed. An insured who has decided to reduce or avoid insurance in a particular respect must be prepared for the situation that arises when a loss occurs. It is indeed a further fact that when a loss occurs the advice or the warning given in the distant past has been forgotten. The blame is laid at the door of the insurer or the agent.

Contrary to popular belief insurers are not automatically suspicious of claimants. They require the claimant to prove the loss and that it is an insured one. For the reasons given earlier many claimants are less than helpful and insurers become embroiled in correspondence, telephone discussions and endless documents. Another fiction is that if a claimant wishes to obtain a satisfactory settlement it is necessary to double all the figures as insurers will reduce them by half as a general practice. Insurers make what they believe to be a reasonable offer for settlement once they have completed their enquiries. They can, however, be persuaded to increase the offer made in many cases. The reason is that claims settlement is more of an art than a science. In the absence of a pure scientific formula they can only work on the basis that has proved successful for some years. If here and there insureds feel aggrieved, then insurers may be prepared to consider that the grievance could be justified and increase the offer for settlement. This does not mean that insurers have tried to deprive the claimant of his or her rights. Indeed, to satisfy the insured they may be persuaded to bend a bit more in his or her favour.

Just as all of those in business look slightly more favourably on the bigger customers, so insurers are influenced by the size of the account they have with the policyholder or, in some cases, the agency. Any influence which can be brought to bear to resolve a dispute favourably is legitimate.

The duty of a claimant is to notify a loss which is a possible insurable one "as soon as possible". This phrase is not clearly defined and will vary according to the situation. In the case of a major fire or a fatal road accident it means within hours. In the first case the insurers will wish to instruct loss adjusters to visit the premises immediately, not only for a preliminary assessment of the loss but also to advise the insured who will wish to keep his or her business running. In the second case insurers will need to instruct local solicitors to represent the insured at the inquest. As such matters often take place within days of the accident urgent action is essential.

At the other extreme the insured with a damaged carpet, a broken window or a dented car may need advice but the question of urgency is on his or her side rather than that of the insurer.

Insurers invariably dispatch a form to the insured which is variously described as a claim form or notice of loss. Dependent on the efficiency of the insurer concerned an insured may be asked for brief details before arrangements are made for the issue of the form. An insured who wishes to have urgent work carried out immediately should press the point to his or her insurers (or the agent concerned). Following upon the serious storm damage in October 1987 many insurers were quite content to issue claim forms to applicants and were taken by surprise many months — or even more than a year — later when substantial accounts arrived with the completed forms. The urgency of many of the situations was such that repairers carried out the work, submitting accounts some time afterwards when they were able to complete the necessary paper work. Insurers who did seek information from applicants for claims forms were able to make rough estimates of the expected losses and take some action at an early stage.

The claim form supplied allows the claimant to provide all the details of the loss so as to enable the insurers to deal with it. Once again, the style of form used will vary between insurers but, in general, many questions are asked. If a large claim is involved correspondence will be at a minimum because queries can be referred to adjusters or assessors. It is expedient in this part of the book to use the term "assessor" to describe anyone instructed by insurers to assist them in settling the claim. The term is used in the case of fire insurance for the professional called by the insured to represent his or her interests.

Insurers wish to know what the loss is, when and where it occurred, how it happened and how much (in monetary terms) is being claimed. If anyone is alleged to have been responsible and if authorities, such as the police and fire service, have been involved, their details are also required.

Professional assistance is necessary when a claim is likely to exceed a pre-decided cost. In many cases it is carried out by an independent professional but in others staff are employed for the purpose. There are fire adjusters, who are mainly independent organisations and motor claims assessors who may be independent or employed by insurers. Independent firms charge fees which, whilst not a percentage of the claim involved, do relate to it due to the effect the size of a loss has on the work involved.

Although insurers claim that outside organisations are completely independent — and, of course, they are — it is a fact that they are paid by, and hope to receive regular work from, insurers. This must have some bearing on their attitude during negotiations. However, there is nothing at all to prevent a claimant instructing assessors to represent his or her interests. If the claim is likely to be substantial, it is advisable. The fees and costs involved cannot form part of the claim under the insurance. Where a claim is being made against a third party, not under the insurance policies held, then professional representation — which might ultimately need to be a legal one — should be considered. In this case the costs involved form part of the claim against the third party insurer.

A claimant should never allow himself or herself to be deflected from submitting a claim to the third party insurer even though his or her own insurer or agent assures him or her that there are agreements between the insurers concerned. The only valid point that arises here, and it has been referred to earlier, is that if there is an urgency, such as to get a vehicle back on to the road, one's own insurers will move faster.

The first action to be taken by insurers is to check if the policy under which the claim is being submitted is in force. If the claim is submitted via the intermediary concerned insurers will assume that the policy is current. Some slips used by intermediaries when submitting claim forms do carry confirmation. In the case of life insurance policies non-payment of premium, within agreed limits, will result in its deduction from the sum insured or surrender value.

At this point if insurers are satisfied from the information that they have that the insurance has expired the insured will be advised accordingly. There should be no delay as the insured must notify the correct insurer. The insurer's letter will probably state that their records do not show that the policy has been renewed. Mindful of possible administrative mistakes by their agents or themselves insurers are very wary. If the insured's reaction suggests that they could be wrong, immediate enquiries will be put in hand.

The way in which claims are settled in the various classes of insurance will be considered separately under the appropriate headings.

If an insured is dissatisfied full details of the complaint should always be sent to a senior official at the insurer's head office. Further steps that can be taken if that action fails to satisfy a claimant are:

(a) Write to the Insurance Ombudsman Bureau (see *Useful Addresses*). Most insurance companies and Lloyd's underwriters are members of the Bureau.

(b) Go to arbitration — some insurers operate a personal insurance

arbitration scheme using independent arbitrators appointed by
the Chartered Institute of Arbitrators. They will review the documents passing between the parties in the light of the ABI Statement of Practice. Arbitration is less formal, quicker and less
expensive than the courts.

(c) Complain to the Consumer Information Department, Association of British Insurers (see *Useful Addresses*).

(d) Write to the British Insurance and Investment Brokers' Association, 130 Fenchurch Street, London, EC3M 5DJ.

(e) Communicate with the Insurance Brokers' Registration Council,
15 St Helen's, London, EC3.

VAT

In settling claims, insurers require to know if the claimant is registered
for VAT. If this is the case then payments made will be net of VAT,
leaving the claimant to obtain the appropriate sum from the revenue
authorities. This will not be applied to private claims, traders not
registered for VAT due to low turnover or exempt rated businesses.
In the case of zero rated commodities the trader will still be able to
claim VAT on input.

Fire claims

As explained earlier, a large fire loss requires urgent notification to
the insurers whereas most fire losses (usually not involving a fire
brigade) can be dealt with by completing a claim form supplied by the
insurers. If the possible loss is substantial the loss adjuster will bring
a claim form with him or her to be completed for submission to
insurers with his or her preliminary report. In smaller cases the
insurers, if they are unsure of the severity of the incident, may ask
their local inspector to visit as soon as possible and help the claimant
in completing a form and solving some of the many problems that can
arise.

The adjuster will, on his or her first visit, try to produce a rough
assessment of the loss. He or she will be interested to discover the
source and, if a fire brigade has attended, liaise with them. In serious

cases, especially in which loss of life has occurred, the police will also be investigating the matter.

The adjuster should have a copy of the insurance policy and will wish to be satisfied that any warranties have been complied with. Such warranties may be concerned with processes or the availability of particular extinguishing equipment. He or she will also try to assess the value of the stock as compared with the sum declared to insurers. If the difference appears to be substantial he or she will undertake a stock check. If the adjuster finds substantial under insurance he or she will advise the insurers that the average clause in the policy operates.

Example

The Manufacturing Company plc insured its stock for £500,000. Following a loss, which was assessed at £200,000, adjusters felt that the stock remaining was higher than they expected. A stock check revealed that there was actually £1M stock at the time of the fire. Average was applied as follows:

$$\frac{\text{Sum insured} \times \text{loss}}{\text{Value at risk}} \qquad \frac{£500,000 \times £200,000}{£1,000,000} = £100,000$$

After satisfying himself that the loss was covered and that there were no breaches of policy terms, the adjuster advised the insurers to pay £100,000. The insured was, therefore, treated as its own insurer for the uninsured portion of the loss.

In dealing with smaller claims, insurers endeavour to assess the value of the loss in a similar way but will not apply average unless the under insurance is blatant enough to warrant it. Often they prefer to obtain the insured's agreement to increase the sum insured, sometimes retrospectively. In cases of stock losses insurers will usually settle on the invoice price. In some cases, as for example in the fashion trade, older stock may be worth substantially less than the invoice price and the lower figure will be negotiated. All the time insurers are conscious that they are providing an indemnity. The insured should not lose as a result of insuring but neither is it equitable that he or she should benefit by receiving more than an indemnity.

Although the term "average" has been used there is more than one form of average (excluding the use of the term in other classes of insurance, such as life and marine, where the meaning is completely different). The type of average condition that we have discussed is called "the pro-rata condition of average". The "special condition of average" applies to agricultural produce on a farm. In this case an average is only applied if the sum insured is less than three-quarters of the value actually at risk at the time of a loss. If it is more, average is not applied. If it is less, then average is calculated as for the pro-rata condition.

The "two conditions of average" apply to larger and more complex risks in which some of the goods are more specifically insured. Thus an insurance on separate buildings and one on "floating" stock throughout the country would be settled by reference to the two conditions of average.

Damage to fixtures and fittings can be resolved by repairers' estimates and, if replacement is required, any betterment resulting will be deducted. For example, if the insured replaces older shelves and counters by new he or she cannot expect "new for old". There is some betterment and he or she will need to accept a reduction in the settlement accordingly.

In the case of household insurances such settlements involve insurers in attempts to value five year-old carpets or ten year-old items of furniture and the much more complex problem of valuing part worn clothing. Most household insurances at the present time depart from the strict principle of indemnity and offer "new for old" cover. At the same time most apply index linking to prevent sums insured deteriorating in an inflationary situation.

Example

The Browns had a household policy which provided an indemnity in respect of fire, theft and many other items. One night the television caught fire and the fire spread to the curtains, the carpet and the settee. Adjusters were instructed and produced the following calculations, based on the insured's claim form:

Television two years old (they could exclude the part that caught fire but it might only be worth a few pence). Cost £400, present price £360—		£200
Carpet ten years old. Cost £400. Present price £500. Salvage value of undamaged remainder £10—	£250–£10 = £240	
Curtains. New. Cost £350—		£350
Settee two years old. Part of a suite costing £1000. All three pieces must be recovered to match. Cost—		£300
		£1090

As the adjuster considered that the sum insured of £15,000 was inadequate and that it should have been double that figure, the insurers offered £545 in settlement. Note that the policy was not on a "new for old" basis. Neither is there usually an average clause in the contract. There is, however, a warranty of full value. In this case the warranty had been breached and the insurers could repudiate liability under the insurance. An offer to settle based on "average" would be a fair compromise.

The insured accepted the points made by the adjuster but disagreed with his calculations and a final settlement of £700 was agreed.

Most of the claims originating from private homes are quite small and to reduce the problems associated with under insurance two new types of insurance policy have been introduced. One has a sum insured based on rebuilding costs on which the premium is calculated. Cover is also included for the contents up to a quite substantial sum. Another type of insurance has no sum insured and the premium is based on the size of the building, its age and location.

Claims may be made against the insured by customers whose goods have been damaged or destroyed whilst in the insured's care. The wording of the insurance policy is wide enough to include such claims.

However, the claimant will probably also have insurance covering the loss. Such claimants should be advised to contact their own insurers but the trader must notify the claim to his or her insurer. In practice such claims are settled by agreement between insurers.

Interruption insurance claims

Except for fairly small incidents, claims under these policies are more complex to settle than most other types of loss. The usual basis of calculation is that of turnover. It is defined in the policy and consists of money paid or payable for the goods sold or services rendered. The turnover can be divided into three parts — variable charges, standing charges and net profit (the latter two together comprising the gross profit of the business).

The period of cover selected should take into consideration the time that will be taken to clear the site, obtain planning permission and replace machinery. There will also be a period before full working has been achieved. Although the usual period is twelve months, periods of up to two years are not unusual. The sum insured should be based on existing figures plus a percentage loading to allow for inflation and an increase in business.

Example

Brushes Ltd had a turnover of £100,000 in the year immediately prior to the fire. In the year following the fire the turnover was £75,000. The variable costs also fell from £40,000 to £30,000 as output fell. There was no effect on standing charges. Thus the differences which would have existed without insurance are seen here:

	Before the fire £	After the fire £
Variable charges	40,000	30,000
Standing charges	40,000	40,000
Net profit	20,000	5,000
Turnover	100,000	75,000

It can be seen that without insurance a drop of £25,000 in turnover has resulted in a fall of £20,000 in net profit. If the trader had effected an interruption (or consequential loss) insurance with sufficient cover, the adjustment would be as follows:

$$\frac{\text{Standing charges} + \text{net profit}}{\text{Turnover}} = \frac{£40,000 + £20,000}{£100,000} = 60\%$$

Shortage in turnover is £25,000 × 60% = £15,000

Add £15,000 to net profit = £20,000

To make the example clear it has been over simplified. The method in general use is the "difference" basis. This defines gross profit by deducting from the sum of the turnover and the amount of the closing stock, the sum of the opening stock and the uninsured working expenses. The uninsured working expenses are usually defined in the policy and are, for example, the cost of raw materials and the wages of the labour force. These would be regarded as reduced or non-existent when production is reduced.

There may be adjustments due to reduction in standing charges and there may also be costs of temporary accommodation. The latter figure, however, needs justifying on the basis that it actually results in a reduced fall in turnover which is less than the cost involved.

For professional persons the income of the business or practice is regarded as gross profit.

There must be insurance in existence which deals with the material damage aspect except where cover is not based on damage or loss at the insured's premises. Examples here are where fire at the supplier's premises is included in the insurance.

There is also cover for engineering losses which can include failure of the public utilities or any sudden and unforeseen damage from any accidental cause. In the case of engineering cover the period is usually only three months with an excess of one or two days.

Water damage

The term is used in relation to overflowing or bursting of water tanks or pipes or damage following storm or flood. If the loss is small the insurers will pay on receipt of a claim form, estimate and account (or detailed account). In more serious cases they may ask for two competitive estimates before settlement.

Where damage is likely to be substantial the insurers should be given more details rather than simply an application for a claim form. This will enable them to instruct specialist adjusters at an early stage. Insurers do like to have the damage seen by an adjuster (who may be a member of their own claims staff), as in fire losses, but appreciate that sometimes urgency precludes this. It is always advisable to retain for inspection damaged materials until insurers have had the opportunity to have them seen. Quite often the advice given by these specialists can save valuable time and also result in producing a better standard of workmanship. In case of substantial loss, surveyors or assessors may be instructed by the insured but such fees cannot form part of the claim. However, many traders have found that professional help, particularly in substantial water damage claims, can pay for itself as a result of improved settlements. The experts appointed by the insurer will negotiate direct with the claimant's own specialists who will recommend the agreed settlement to the claimant for acceptance.

As the insured has both a common law and a contractual liability to do all that is possible to protect the subject of the insurance, urgent or "first aid" work should always be put in hand. Subject to retaining the materials, as mentioned above, further damage or deterioration must not be allowed to occur. Insurers cannot raise an objection to a reasonable course of action.

The insurance policy is not a maintenance contract and insurers will attempt to reduce substantial claims by excluding those costs which they think are more properly maintenance. The problem will not arise in reasonably new premises but, in the case of older ones, proof of good maintenance will be necessary to defeat such allegations.

An excess usually applies in respect of losses caused by bursting or overflowing of water tanks, apparatus or pipes, and storm, tempest or flood claims.

Theft claims

Unless a claim form has been supplied with the policy an immediate application should be made to the agent or insurer. At the same time the police should be notified. Anyone claiming against the trader should be advised to contact their own insurers (if there is any possibility of cover in existence) but insurers must still be advised accordingly.

As in fire claims the degree of urgency in notification will be based on the size of the loss. Policy conditions require the insured to take all possible steps to recover the loss. This means notifying the police. Insurers are particularly interested in the report made by the police as to the cause of the loss. The police report will indicate whether they have seen evidence to indicate that the loss resulted from "forcible and violent" entry or exit. This evidence may well be crucial in a business claim.

The police will require details of losses sustained and insurers usually submit details of the claim notified to them for comparison. This does not mean that a claimant is precluded from listing items on the claim form that were overlooked when advising the police. It is a well known fact that many items are not missed until actually required, which may be some time after a robbery. Any list given to the police should be stated as a "provisional" one.

Insurers have been faced with supplementary lists of losses after settlement and the insured must then rely on their goodwill if a further payment is to be made.

The insured may have a liability as bailee (because goods are entrusted to him or her for repair or storage) but the claimant may also have insurance in existence. The trader's policy cover may differ from that of the claimant in that it will be worded to protect the trader against claims made against him or her. A claimant would need to attribute some degree of blame to the trader to recover the loss from the trader's insurance. In practice insurers have agreements or reach an agreement in specific cases. It is no defence for a trader to claim that he or she took the same care with a customer's property as with his or her own. The courts have decided that a trader's own standards may not be good enough!

Third party claims

Claims may be made against a trader which are covered by an employers' or public liability insurance. In some instances the matter can be dealt with under a family (or personal) liability insurance or a professional indemnity, or even product liability insurance. There is a temptation to get involved in correspondence before seeking the help

of insurers, particularly when the insured is indignant about the impu-
tations contained in the letter. This must be avoided. The action which
must be taken, other than simply acknowledging the letter or claim,
is to communicate with the insurers, sending them all the documents
received. It is not advisable to inform the claimant of these actions as,
in some cases, insurers may wish to remain in the background —
claims values seem to escalate if it is known that an insurer is involved.

Where the claim is made verbally the claimant should be asked to
put it into writing. No discussion should take place other than a simple
denial once it is clear that a claim is being submitted or pursued.

Some insurers have found that they can deal with small claims by
authorising the insured to arrange a settlement with a claimant. No
mention is made of the existence of insurance and a suitably worded
form of discharge is provided by the insurers. The importance of the
wording lies in the possibility that a claimant can pursue a claim
further using the insured's payment as an admission of liability.

Example

Following an incident in which a customer fell down in a shop
and sustained minor injuries a claim was submitted for damage
to a pair of shoes and tights. The total claim was £30. After
a brief conversation with insurers, the insured contacted the
claimant and negotiated settlement at £25 and made a payment.

The insurers sent the insured a discharge wording to copy
onto his or her own notepaper for signature by the claimant.

The wording used was:

"I agree to accept the sum of £25 (twenty five pounds) in full
and final settlement of all claims in respect of the incident on
or about 25 January 1989 in Smith's Grocery Supermarket,
1 High Street, Nowhere. Such settlement being made without
admission of liability.

Signature ....   Witnessed by ....
Address ....   Name ....
....   Address ....
....   Occupation ....
Date ....

Practice varies among insurers in the use of forms of discharge. Some do not use them at all, others issue a cheque with a suitable discharge wording on the reverse and many insurers have a form of discharge signed prior to the issue of a cheque or sent with a cheque.

The practice of allowing the insured to become involved in the settlement is fading. There are two reasons for this. The first is that if the claimant finally accepts what he or she believes to be an unfair settlement the insured is distanced from the situation and his or her goodwill may not suffer as a result. The second reason is that the public as a whole are much more conscious of their rights and the existence of insurance. In fact the percentage of claims that are pursued rises annually. It is, in those circumstances, an advantage for insurers to negotiate directly with the third party from the start.

In addition to legal action, which has become somewhat easier since the introduction of the small claims procedure in the county court, many more facilities exist for the claimant to influence prompt settlements. These include the press, local radio and television. Whilst carefully investigating all third party claims insurers are conscious of the special need to protect the insured's goodwill.

Insurer's investigate all potential claims. In some cases care has to be taken. Employers are asked to complete a report following any accident involving an employee. In the majority of these no further activity takes place. However, there are those that are found to be more serious than originally thought and a claim is notified against the employer.

Insurers are in some difficulty here. If, on receiving a report, they investigate, which could include photographs of the scene of the incident and witness statements from fellow employees, the fact of their interest could instigate a claim. If they fail to investigate while the facts are still clear in everyone's minds they may face difficulties at a later stage.

In some cases insurers will appoint consultant assessors to investigate on their behalf. In many cases the insurer's own staff deal with the investigations until such time as solicitors are involved on behalf of the claimant. Dependent on the size of the claim the insurers may attempt to effect a settlement or pass the file to their own insurers. Discussions can be protracted and, if eventually reaching the High Court, take two or more years to be heard.

If an incident involves personal injury insurers will require that the claimant is examined by a medical consultant appointed by them.

They will pay the fee and the travelling expenses of the claimant for this purpose. In small claims insurers have been prepared to accept a letter from the claimant's own GP detailing the extent of the injuries and the period of incapacity.

Often, following a settlement, the insured states his or her objection to the insurers, probably feeling that he or she is personally being "found guilty" of the allegations made against him or her by the third party. This is not the case. The insurers will always inform the insured of the specific allegations made, but retain the right to settle in the best possible way. This often means settling a doubtful or excessive claim, rather than getting involved in legal costs in the High Court. There is an element of risk in litigation that insurers must balance against the benefits of a settlement.

Motor insurance claims

Most insurers separate motor claims into "own damage" and "third party".

The first, involving staff who will, if necessary, arrange for the vehicle to be seen by a motor claims assessor employed by them or by an independent assessor whose fee they will pay. Except where they provide insureds with the names of recommended repairers, the vehicle may be taken to any competent body shop. At the same time the motor insurers must be notified and they will issue a claim form. In some cases agents prefer to be involved at this stage.

Most motor insurance policies state a sum up to which the insured may issue his or her own instructions for repairs, submitting an estimate to the insurers and sending the paid account for reimbursement.

If the damage is substantial the insurers should be advised when requesting a claim form so that assessors may be instructed immediately. If there is a delay and the insured instructs repairs he or she must be responsible for the costs until the insurers have approved the estimate and have a satisfactory claim form. A mere statement that they have no objection to the work being put in hand means just that. They are not yet accepting liability for the repair costs.

If work is to commence before the insurers have had the opportunity to inspect the vehicle all damaged parts must be retained by the repairers. The insurers will pay the repair costs authorised less:

(a) any policy excess, which must be paid directly to the repairers
    by the insured;
(b) VAT if the insured is registered for this;
(c) any agreed contribution towards repairs. This may arise if there
    is "betterment" involved. Replacement of a worn tyre by a new
    one, repainting and replacement of rusted parts are all likely to
    involve some contribution from the insured. Indemnity requires
    insurers to replace damaged parts with equivalent ones that are
    no better and no worse. This is impractical so that new parts
    are fitted and a reasonable contribution may be calculated for
    wear and tear.

Even if a third party is liable it is advantageous to have the vehicle
repairs paid by insurers rather than to submit a claim against the third
party or his or her insurers. It is a legal requirement that the driver
must give his or her insurance details if he or she has damaged a
vehicle, property or caused personal injury. Thus it has now become
easier to recover from the third party. However, unless a third party
is prepared to deal with a claim against him or her personally the
insurers will prefer to await a report.

Insurers do have agreements and, in most cases, the insured's no
claim discount is protected. However, if liability is clear (a further
hurdle, if the claimant is pressing a third party the insured cannot be
compelled to go to his or her own insurer. If the claimant does not
have a comprehensive motor insurance he or she will have to claim
the cost of repairs from the third party or his or her insurers.

Drivers must give their insurance details after an accident. If the
third party driver is uninsured a claim could, in certain circumstances,
be made to the Motor Insurers' Bureau.

The procedure in submitting a claim against the third party is:
(a) write to the third party (or his or her insurers, if they are known,
    stating the third party's policy number) holding him or her
    responsible and sending an estimate for repairs. If an estimate
    is not available the letter should be sent informing them of the
    damage and saying that an estimate will follow. If instructions
    are given to repairers, damaged parts should be retained;
(b) notify the insurers that a claim has been submitted against the
    third party or his or her insurers.

In the event of theft the police and insurers should be notified. As
many stolen vehicles are found abandoned shortly afterwards,
insurers delay settlement in these cases for some weeks. Cover varies

in cases in which property is stolen from private cars. Usually, if the policy is comprehensive, there is some cover for small items of clothing or personal effects. Actual details will be found on the policy.

Stolen vehicles or property recovered after a claim has been settled are the property of the insurers who will usually offer them to the insured in exchange for the return of the claims payment. Any damage on a vehicle will be deducted from the refund. In most cases the missing vehicle has been replaced and the assessors sell the vehicle on behalf of the insurers. Sometimes recovered property has a sentimental value and an insured may be pleased to "buy back" items recovered.

Transit claims in respect of goods stolen from a vehicle should also be notified to the police and the insurers must be advised. If an alarm has been stipulated the insurers will wish to have confirmation that it was in effect at the time of the incident. Insurers are unhappy about situations in which it appears that the vehicle was not properly locked at the time of a loss. It is more than likely that they may refuse an indemnity to the insured.

Help in recovering uninsured losses is available from the motoring organisations for members and there are also uninsured loss recovery services prepared to negotiate. Many intermediaries offer membership of a recovery and legal advice scheme to clients at inception and renewal of insurance policies. There are six or seven specialists in this field and premiums are quite low — around £7 or £8 a year. In some cases intermediaries are charged a premium and add their fee; in other cases brokers pay for the services and are allowed a commission. Some private claims assessors handle recoveries for a fee, or solicitors may be instructed.

Claim forms are designed to provide the insurers with full details of the accident, the use to which the vehicle was being put and the driver at the time of the incident. Obviously, insurers will wish to be satisfied that only an authorised person was driving or in charge (if the vehicle was parked) at the time of the accident.

They will then wish to check that the use was covered by the policy.

All drivers should be required to carry prepared forms or similar material so that accurate completion of the claim form will be simple. If drivers are provided with a small clipboard with some spare sheets of paper and accident forms (and to which a ballpoint pen is attached) the process at the scene of the accident will not be a problem.

An example of the information required at the scene of an accident, which could be listed on an accident form, is as follows:

(a) name and address of the driver and owner of any third party vehicle (or vehicles);
(b) name and address of the third party insurers and policy number (or numbers);
(c) details of the third party vehicle (or vehicles), eg registration mark, make, model and colour;
(d) name, number and station of any police officer attending;
(e) name and address of independent witnesses (these would not be with or in the vehicle of a third party);
(f) details of injured parties;
(g) date, time, weather and road conditions;
(h) a drawing showing the width of the road, measurements and how the accident occurred.

Photographs are valuable and, if possible, should be taken as soon as possible after the accident.

The third party claims section of the motor claims department deals with claims made against their insureds.

Overseas accidents are much more difficult to deal with. Many insurers have offices or agencies abroad, as do the motoring organisations. However, the law varies from country to country and language problems add to the difficulties. Many insurers issue a "European Accident Statement" to policyholders who apply for an overseas insurance extension and certificate (usually referred to as a "green card").

The initial sections of the form deal with the incident and the place and there are two sections, each of eleven questions, which relate to the details of the parties involved, their vehicle, damage and insurance details. Question 12 offers a choice of 17 possibilities relating to the incident to ascertain exactly what sort of manoeuvre, if any, each of the parties was engaged in doing. Question 13 requires a drawing and question 14 requests remarks by both parties, followed by their signatures.

If both parties complete and sign the form it can be sent to the insurers. If the other party refuses to become involved, the insured can complete and return the form to the insurers knowing that he or she has supplied all the information that is considered relevant. Although in use for over fifteen years in Europe, many Europeans are puzzled by some of its "simple" questions. The advice is to take great care not to tick any answer unless it exactly fits the situation.

Motor Insurers' Bureau

Many discussions took place between insurers and Government departments following the introduction of compulsory third party motor insurance in 1930. Originally insurance was in respect of unlimited indemnity against third party personal injury, excluding passengers in or on the insured vehicle. Later, passengers were included in the compulsory cover required. At the end of 1988 limited property damage cover was added, following a European Community directive.

One problem concerned ineffective insurances. These were situations in which the insurers refused to indemnify their insured following proof of non-disclosure or other breaches of the terms of the insurance. An amendment to the Road Traffic Act in 1934 required insurers to pay third party personal injury claims that arose with a right of recovery against their insured in these circumstances.

Other matters troubled the Government because, in spite of compulsory insurance, there were still occasions in which an injured member of the public could not be compensated. A committee report was shelved until after the second world war, when insurers and the Government agreed on a voluntary code. This became the Motor Insurers' Bureau, financed by most of the motor insurers in the British insurance market.

Since the addition of compulsory third party property insurance from 31.12.88 the Motor Insurers' Bureau will pay for property damage up to a maximum of £250,000 per claim (but excluding the first £175 of each claim). Damage caused by untraced drivers is not included nor are claims which can be met from other existing insurances.

The present position with regard to claims which are unsatisfied by motor insurers is as follows:

(a) If insurers refuse an indemnity due to a breach of utmost good faith or policy terms, they must pay the third party claims. They then have a right of recovery against their insured. Repayment by insureds in these circumstances is very unlikely.

(b) If there is no policy in force, if the insurer has gone into liquidation, or if there is no insurance in respect of the person driving the vehicle (eg insurance is restricted to the insured only but someone else was driving) the Bureau will deal with the claim. As the Bureau does not maintain a claims staff members agree to act on its behalf when requested. If they have an insurance contract which does not cover the loss they are called the "insurer concerned" and deal with the claim as if they are the insurers of the motorist. They will be reimbursed by the Bureau from its funds. During negotiations the motorist will be required to sign an agreement to repay the Bureau's outlay (except in cases in which the insurers are in liquidation). In many cases the offending motorist may face his or her own repair costs, fines and, perhaps, imprisonment. In these circumstances it is even less likely that the Bureau will receive reimbursement.

(c) Where the motorist cannot be traced, the "hit and run" case, the Bureau will undertake to pay the claim and instruct one of its members to act for it during the investigations necessary to establish that a motor vehicle appears to have been the cause of the accident and the driver of that vehicle liable to pay a claim against him or her. The agreed loss will be paid from the Bureau's own funds. Claims will not be dealt with in respect of property damage.

(d) The Bureau will act on behalf of foreigners visiting Great Britain who are insured by a member of an overseas bureau. Similarly, if a British national travelling abroad is involved in an accident the overseas bureau will act on behalf of his or her insurers. Motorists are issued with the overseas insurance certificate ("green card") by their own insurers. Most insurers charge an additional premium for the overseas cover granted although third party cover to meet European Community requirements exists in the absence of the certificate.

Most motor insurers in Great Britain have branches or agencies in overseas countries who will act on their behalf. This avoids the necessity to use the services of the Motor Insurers' Bureau and its overseas counterparts.

It should be noted that the use of the "green card" scheme is not restricted to members of the European Community. Drivers not able to provide the necessary insurance proofs to suit the requirements of any country that they are visiting will be charged for short period motor insurance at the frontier.

Claims settling agreements

Insurers have a variety of agreements with each other to facilitate prompt settlement of claims and also to reduce correspondence, negotiation, disagreements and litigation. Although most agreements are in a standard form, each insurer negotiates all agreements individually with other insurers.

Knock for knock agreements

The most well known agreement is the "knock for knock" arrangement. In this type of agreement each insurer agrees to pay for damages to its insured's car subject to the policy including cover in respect of damage to the insured vehicle. The agreement usually applies in respect of collision, attempt to avoid collision, loading or unloading and goods falling from vehicles. It also deals with claims following accidents whilst the vehicle is at a repairer as dual insurance exists.

When an insured drives a vehicle belonging to someone else (most policies provide an indemnity restricted to third party cover only) who also holds an insurance which allows that other person to drive, there is dual insurance. Both policies will have excluded cover because of the existence of another insurance. In practice, both insurers share the third party claim.

All settlements under the knock for knock agreement take into consideration the existence of excesses. Insureds are not party to these agreements and can claim uninsured losses from the third party insurers.

Third party sharing agreements

If, following an accident between two vehicles, a third party is injured or third party property is damaged then, without considering liability, the insurers of the vehicles share the third party loss. As such agreement could, in theory, be unlimited, each agreement is subject to a previously agreed upper limit.

Common law agreement

Where such an agreement exists, if an insured holds both a motor insurance and an employers' liability insurance the latter meets claims for which an employer could be liable even though the loss was caused by a motor vehicle. An example would be a claim by an injured employee against a driver employed by the same firm.

Immobile property agreement

Insurers may enter into agreements with other insurers and local authorities in respect of damage to property (eg walls, street lamps, traffic bollards — but not vehicles) caused by vehicles. The usual provision is that vehicle insurers pay two-thirds of the costs of repairs or replacement.

Motor (fire) agreements

The object of these agreements is to avoid an insurer being liable for loss or damage to many vehicles if fire in one vehicle spreads to others. Where vehicles are insured against fire each insurer will pay his or her own claim and not seek reimbursement against the insurer of the vehicle from which the fire spread. This would be subject to the insurance cover including fire.

There are other agreements in existence and variations of those listed above.

CHAPTER 8

Risk Management

Large businesses have on many occasions questioned the costs of insuring. On the one side they accept the benefit of an annual and fairly predictable business expense — the premium. On the other they consider the fact that insurers are in business for profit and that they would not wish to contribute to it. They, therefore, decide that they will retain as much of the insurance risk as they can do safely so as to reduce their outlay in premium. Some businesses look back over the years and see a regular pattern of claims, many of which they feel they could absorb (as an example, accident damage repairs to commercial vehicles).

Risk management consists of assessing all the risks of a business, not necessarily only insurable ones, and making decisions about handling them individually. Some may be insured, some retained and some ignored. The difference between retaining and ignoring is the difference between setting up a fund to meet losses and accepting that certain losses can be met out of revenue.

The risk of not insuring is that of heavy losses occurring and requiring additional finance from other money within the business. The advantages insurers have over most businesses is their ability to spread losses over many insureds throughout this country and abroad. They have expert advice available which can help to improve risks. All this is denied to the business carrying its own risks.

The entry to a scheme of risk management is by first of all selecting those risks which the business feels it can handle without insurance. This could mean accepting larger excesses under most of the existing policies. Paying for third party insurance for motor vehicles, perhaps fire and theft for expensive vehicles only, but not having accidental damage insurance on any vehicles. In effect the business is retaining the better risks and insuring those in which losses are more likely to occur and, when they do, may be too much for the newly set up fund to bear. If their planning is correct there will be a saving but, if it is wrong, the business will need to finance the losses from money earmarked for other purposes or from profits.

However, the concept of risk management is lost if no separate fund is set up to meet these losses. Many local authorities who, over the years, did not effect insurances against loss by theft found that replacement reduced capital improvements by depleting funds available.

If the risk management plan is successful funds will be built up to be invested and retained against future losses. Unfortunately, businesses will not have the insurer's tax advantage of being able to carry forward untaxed reserves. This is one reason why large businesses set up "captive" insurers and pay their premiums to them. In this way they obtain the tax benefit of being able to charge premiums as outgoings. The captive is taxed as an insurer.

CHAPTER 9

Insurance in Inner Cities

For some years difficulty has been experienced by traders in inner cities who wish to insure. In 1986 the Association of British Insurers launched an initiative which involved cooperation with the Department of Employment. The object of the activity was to investigate enquiries originating from individual businesses in Government Task Force and City Action Team inner city areas. The responsibility for inner cities coordination is now under the control of the Department of Trade and Industry. In 1987 the local authorities in Lambeth, Leeds, Manchester and Birmingham were included in the initiative.

Insurers who are members of the ABI are supporting the scheme and making insurance available. Contact points have been established and questionnaires will be sent on application by businesses experiencing difficulty. The completed questionnaire will be used to assist in solving the trader's problem. The initiative is intended as a last resort.

How to obtain information

If there is an existing policy with an insurer who is a member of the ABI, the Association will endeavour to assist. If new insurances cannot be placed through insurers or intermediaries the Association may be approached for advice. Lloyd's cases are taken up directly with the Lloyd's broker involved and not the ABI contact point.

There is no guarantee of cover and insurers will not depart from their normal commercial criteria in the rating of risks. This means that, although a competitive rate is always quoted by insurers, the rate will be the normal rate for the risk and the area.

How to obtain advice and assistance

The initiative also provides for surveys to be carried out and advice given for risk improvement. Insurers will use their own surveyors where possible but otherwise the ABI contact point will make arrangements for a free survey.

The ABI points out that it is essential that enquirers approach insurers and intermediaries direct until the point is reached in which they feel that they cannot obtain cover. There are risks that insurers do not find attractive and in those cases extra effort is needed to obtain quotations.

Once the trader feels that cover cannot be obtained, a questionnaire should be obtained from the Task Force, City Action Team or local authority for the area. The completed form should be returned to the office of issue which will check it for accuracy and completeness before forwarding it to the ABI contact point.

On receipt of the questionnaire the ABI will investigate the matter and try to arrange for an insurer to quote. It will then report back to the office of issue (the Task Force, City Action Team or local authority) on the results of its investigations.

The addresses

City Action Teams — contact points

Birmingham:
P J Matthews
DTI, Room 719
Ladywood House
Stephenson Street
Birmingham
B1 4DT
Tel: 021-632 4111 ext. 589

Liverpool:
Mr J Warnock
Department of Employment
Graeme House
Derby Square

Liverpool
L2 7SU
Tel: 051-277 4111 ext. 450

London:
Mr B Horner
Manpower Services Commission
Room 417
236 Grays Inn Road
London
WC1X 8HL
Tel: 01-278 0363 ext. 4345

Manchester:
Mr J Law
DTI, Room 706
Sunley Tower
Piccadilly Plaza
Manchester
M1 4BA
Tel: 061-236 2171 ext. 612

Newcastle/Gateshead:
Ms B Grey
Manpower Services Commission
Broadacre House
Market Street
Newcastle
NE1 6HH
Tel: 091-232 6181

Task Force — contact points

London — North Peckham:
Mr D Levy
2nd Floor
72 Rye Lane
London
SE15 5DQ
Tel: 01-358 9018

Doncaster:
Mr D Wilkinson
Room 110 Kingsway House
Hallgate
Doncaster
DN1 3PP
Tel: 0302 329052

North Kensington:
Mr C Francis
2 Acklam Road
London
W10 5QZ
Tel: 01-960 8455

Hartlepool:
Mr B Pollard
c/o Dept of Employment
21 Roly Road
Hartlepool
TS24 8AX
Tel: 0429 272227

Spitalfields/Tower Hamlets:
Mr I Rosser
3rd Floor, Cityside House
40 Adler Street
London
E1 1EE
Tel: 01-377 1866

Leicester — Highfields:
Mr R Fenley
23 Egginton Street
Leicester
LE5 5BD
Tel: 0533 552248

Birmingham — Handsworth:
Mr M Tovey
227 Lozells Road
Birmingham
B19 1RJ
Tel: 021-523 3241

Leeds — Chapeltown/Harehills:
Mr J Lister
158/160 Chapeltown Road
Leeds
LS7 4EE
Tel: 0532 626202

Manchester — Moss Side:
Mr P Shilliday
7 Parisian Way
Moss Lane East
Manchester
M15 5NQ
Tel: 061-226 8899

Bristol — St Pauls:
Mr B Cornish
189a Newfoundland Road
Bristol
B5 9NT
Tel: 0272 550205

Coventry:
Mr D Player
Room 415
4 Copthall House
Station Square
Coventry
CV1 2PP
0203 24310

Middlesbrough:
Mr J Rundle
1st Floor
132/134 Borough Road
Middlesborough
TS1 2ES
Tel: 0642 221162

Nottingham:
Mr I Samways
c/o Dept of Trade and Industry
Chalfont Drive
Nottingham
NG8 3SS
Tel: 0602 291111 ext. 2645

Preston:
Mr H Eastwood
8th Floor, Victoria House
Omskirk Road
Preston
PR1 2DX
Tel: 0772 201770 ext. 18

Rochdale:
Mr M Clarke
c/o Job Centre
Octagon House
Yorkshire Street
Rochdale
OL16 1BW
Tel: 0706 523623

Wolverhampton:
Mr F Pickerill
50/54 Worcester Street
Wolverhampton
WV2 4LL
Tel: 0902 24005

Local authority — contact points

Birmingham:
Ms T Marks
Economic Development Unit
Birmingham Council
The Council House
Birmingham
B1 1BB
Tel: 021-235 4873

Lambeth/Brixton:
Mr R K Lewis
Asst. Director Town Planning
and Economic Development
Courtenay House
New Park Road
Brixton
London
SW2 4DU
Tel: 01-674 9844 ext. 129

Leeds:
Mr M Zahir
Industry and Estates
East Leeds Area Team
Seacroft Skills Centre
Lime Wood Approach
Leeds
LS14 1NG
Tel: 0532 731203

Manchester:
Mr C Fishwick
Economic Development Dept.
City of Manchester Industrial
Development Unit
St James Building
Oxford Street
Manchester
M1 6FL
Tel: 061-234 1252

CHAPTER 10

National Enterprise Insurance Scheme

This scheme is designed to provide those starting a new business and those already established with the assistance of Business in the Community or one of the enterprise agencies with access to an insurance market that understands their particular problems and can offer cover at competitive terms.

A brochure providing details of the cover available (generally as in the packages described in this book) and a brief form for contact is available from the coordinating Lloyd's brokers at the addresses given below. Their response will be to communicate with the applicant for more details after which they will obtain a suitable quotation. If the quotation is acceptable they will supply a proposal form after which they guarantee the delivery of a policy within 28 days. Credit facilities are also offered.

The scheme organisers will be writing to all existing businesses and local enterprise boards. Specific and general enquiries can be made to the contact addresses.

Write via Freepost, telephone or fax the contact in the enterprise departments at the following addresses:

Stafford Knight and Co Ltd
4/5 London Wall Buildings
London
EC2B 2ES
Tel: 01-628 3135
Fax: 01-638 2510

Stafford Knight and Co Ltd
Crown House
Armley Road
Leeds
LS12 2YQ
Tel: 0532 448481
Fax: 0532 420953

Stafford Knight (Eastern) Ltd
Clarendon House
North Station Road
Colchester
CO1 1BR
Tel: 0206 764567
Fax: 0206 763536

Useful Addresses

Association of British Insurers
Head Office
Aldermary House
Queen Street
London EC4N 1TT
Tel: 01-248 4477

Regional Offices

London and South East:
Aldermary House (see above)

Eastern:
Rouen House
Rouen Road
Norwich
NR1 1RB
Tel: 0603 666251

Midlands:
Prudential Buildings
St Philips House
Birmingham
B3 2PW
Tel: 021-236 6761

North West:
208 Royal Exchange
Manchester
M2 7BT
Tel: 061-832 9208

Liverpool and North Wales:
4th Floor
5 Castle Street
Liverpool
L2 4SW
Tel: 051-236 7458

Yorkshire and Humberside:
Yorkshire House
Greek Street
Leeds
LS1 5SX
Tel: 0532 441655

Southern:
Prudential Buildings
Above Bar Street
Southampton
SO1 0FG
Tel: 0703 226356

South-West and South Wales:
Transom House
Victoria Street
Bristol
Tel: 0272-297 478

Scotland:
Third Floor
30 Gordon Street
Glasgow
G1 3PU
Tel: 041-226 3905

Loss Prevention Council
140 Aldersgate Street
London
EC1A 4HY
Tel: 01-606 1050

**Financial Intermediaries,
Managers and Brokers
Regulatory Association
(FIMBRA)**
Hertsmere House
Marsh Wall
London
E14 9RW
Tel: 01-538 8860

**National Supervisory Council
for Intruder Alarms**
Queensgate House
140 Cookham Road
Maidenhead
Berkshire
SL6 8AJ
Tel: 0628 37512

Northern Ireland:
Scottish Provident Building
Donegal Square West
Belfast
BT1 6JE
Tel: 0232 249176

Northern:
12 Moseley Street
Newcastle Upon Tyne
NE1 1DE
Tel: 091-261 4844

**Life Assurance and Unit Trust
Regulatory Organisation
(LAUTRO)**
Centre Point
103 New Oxford Street
London
WC1A 1QH
Tel: 01-379 0444

**British Insurance and
Investment Brokers' Association**
BIIBA House
130 Fenchurch Street
London
EC3M 5DJ
Tel: 01-623 9043

**Insurance Brokers' Registration
Council**
15 St Helen's
London
EC3

Insurance Ombudsman Bureau
31 Southampton Row
London
WC1B 5HJ
Tel: 01-242 8613

Glossary of Terms

These are brief explanations of some of the terms that have been used in the book.

acceptance A written offer of life insurance. On payment of the premium the insurance is in force.

accident insurance All classes of insurance other than life, fire and marine.

actuary He or she is employed by life insurers to calculate the premiums.

agent This is a legal term for an intermediary. In insurance practice he or she acts between the insurer and the insured.

annuity A regular payment in return for a lump sum payment.

assessor Professional person employed by an insured to look after his or her interests following a loss.

assurance Early term which means the same as "insurance". Still used extensively in life insurance and at Lloyd's.

average Term which has more than one meaning in insurance. In general insurance it is a means of reducing the claim payment in the event of under insurance.

bonus Allocation of part of the profits made by a life insurer to a "with profits" policyholder.

broker An intermediary who is registered under the Insurance Brokers (Registration) Act 1977.

brokerage Commission paid to an insurance broker.

business interruption Sometimes called consequential loss or loss of profits. A further loss arising as a result of material damage to insured property.

certificate Document issued by an insurer confirming the existence of insurance cover as required by law.

claim Injury loss or damage affecting the insured and being a liability under an insurance policy.

coinsurance   Sharing of risk among insurers.

combined insurance   A package covering a number of insurable risks.

commission   Payment made to an insurance intermediary by an insurer in return for arranging an insurance.

condition   Terms of the contract. Most insurance policies contain written conditions.

cover note   Written evidence of insurance issued prior to the policy document.

days of grace   Period of time after the expiry of an insurance during which insurers are prepared to accept the premium. A claim occurring during the days of grace will be met if the premium is paid before the expiry of the days allowed. General insurances usually allow 15 days of grace and life insurances one month.

endorsement   Written evidence of a change in the insurance as shown in the policy.

endowment   Life insurance policy which pays a lump sum at the expiry of an agreed term of years or at death if previous.

ex gratia   A payment made by insurers when no liability exists under the insurance contract.

excess   The first part of a loss for which the insured agrees to accept liability. It could be voluntary (in return for a discount) or compulsory.

franchise   Sum for which the insured is liable in the event of a loss. If the loss exceeds the franchise insurers will pay the claim in full. Note how it differs from an excess which must be paid.

indemnity   Basic object of insurance. After a loss insurers attempt to put the insured in the same financial position as he or she was in prior to the loss. Does not apply to life insurance and personal accident insurance.

industrial life   Life insurance in which premiums are collected from the homes of policyholders at weekly or monthly intervals.

insurable interest   Person effecting insurance must have legally recognised relationship with the person, property or liability insured.

insurance   A way of providing financial protection against many types of loss.

insured   The person who effects the insurance and who is to be protected by it.

insurer   An individual or organisation that accepts insurance risks.

intermediary   See *agent*.

knock for knock agreement Agreement between motor insurers to pay the costs of repairs to their insured's vehicles following an accident without contesting liability.

Lloyd's Provides facilities for insurance brokers to offer insurances to underwriters.

loss adjuster An independent qualified person used by insurers to settle claims arising.

loss assessor See *assessor*.

material fact Any fact which will influence the decision of an underwriter in deciding whether to accept a risk offered and, if accepting, at what rate of premium.

maturity The date the sum insured under a life insurance policy will be paid.

misrepresentation A false statement of a material fact.

mutual company Owned by the policyholders.

non-disclosure Withholding of a material fact.

paid-up policy The term, or similar terms, refers to a situation in which the insured has ceased to pay the premiums on a life insurance and insurers have arranged to pay the value to date at maturity.

policy Written document which is evidence of the insurance contract.

premium Payment by the insured for the insurance.

proposer Person or business seeking insurance.

proposal form Printed form containing a series of questions to be completed by someone proposing for insurance.

pro-rata Calculation of a premium based on the exact proportion of the year's insurance.

proprietary company Company owned by shareholders.

proximate cause The direct cause of the loss without the interference of a new and uninsured cause.

reinstatement Usually the restoration of an existing property although the term is sometimes used when a claim is settled without deduction for "wear and tear".

reinsurance The practice of insurers placing part of a risk or parts of all risks with another insurer. The insured neither knows of, nor is party to, the arrangement.

renewal Continuation of insurance for a further period of time.

representation Statements made during negotiations for insurance.

risk The possibility of the loss occurring. Sometimes used to refer to the premises insured.

short period rate   Charge for insurance which is more than an exact proportion of the annual premium.

subrogation   Legal right of an insurer who has paid a loss to recover, if possible, from a third party.

surrender   Cancellation of a life insurance for payment.

underwriter   Person who decides on acceptance of a risk and who rates the premium if accepting.

utmost good faith   The requirement that a proposer for insurance must divulge all he or she knows about the risk proposed for insurance.

warranty   Fundamental term of an insurance contract. Breach by the insured entitles insurers to repudiate.

Index